THE HERITAGE OF JAPANESE CIVILIZATION

The Heritage
of Japanese Civilization

Albert M. Craig

Harvard University

Prentice
Hall

Upper Saddle River, New Jersey 07458

Library of Congress Cataloging-in-Publication Data

CRAIG, ALBERT M.
The heritage of Japanese civilization / Albert M. Craig.
p. cm.
Includes index.
ISBN 0-13-576612-5
1. Japan—History. 2. Japan—Historical geography. 3. Japan—Civilization. I. Title.
DS835.C73 2003
952—dc21

2002074955

VP, Editorial Director: *Charlyce Jones Owen*
Acquisitions Editor: *Charles Cavaliere*
Editorial Assistant: *Adrienne Paul*
AVP, Director of Production and Manufacturing: *Barbara Kittle*
Editorial Production/Supervision and Interior Design: *Judith Winthrop*
Project Liaison: *Louise Rothman*
Prepress and Manufacturing Manager: *Nick Sklitisis*
Prepress and Manufacturing Buyer: *Sherry Lewis*
Marketing Director: *Beth Mejia*
Marketing Manager: Claire Bitting
Manager, Production/Formatting and Art: *Guy Ruggiero*
Cartographers: *Carto-Graphics, Mirella Signoretto*
Cover Design: *Kiwi Design*
Photo Researcher: *Elaine Soares*
Cover Art: Tosa (attributed to): People along the river. Detail from screen representing the River Festival. 17th CE.
Painting on paper. EO 61 MG 25144. Photo: Amaudet. Musee des Arts Asiatiques-Guimet, Paris, France.
Reunion des Musees Nationaux/Art Resource, NY.

This book was set in 10/12.5 Caslon 540 by DM Cradle Associates
and was printed and bound by Hamilton.
The cover was printed by Phoenix Color Corporation.

© 2003 by Prentice-Hall
A Unit of Pearson Education
Upper Saddle River, New Jersey 07458

Printed in the United States of America
10 9 8 7 6 5 4 3 2 1

ISBN 0-13-576612-5

Pearson Education Ltd., *London*
Pearson Education Australia Pty. Limited, *Sydney*
Pearson Education Singapore, Pte. Ltd.
Pearson Education North Asia Ltd, *Hong Kong*
Pearson Education Canada Ltd., *Toronto*
Pearson Education de Mexico, S.A. de C.V.
Pearson Education—Japan, *Tokyo*
Pearson Education Malaysia, Pte. Ltd.
Pearson Education, *Upper Saddle River, New Jersey*

For John and Paul Craig

Contents

4
Modern Japan, 1853–1945   93

Maps

Documents

Preface

The long and rich history of Japan was marked by three major transitions, each initiated by contact with a more advanced technology and different culture.

The first transition was from a hunting and gathering society that had been in place for thousands of years to an agricultural and metal-working society of villagers and local aristocrats. The transition began in about 300 BCE, when northeast Asian peoples, crossing from the Korean peninsula to Japan, introduced the new technologies and their accompanying culture.

In the second transition the Japanese actively reached out for the technologies, writing system, and culture of China, and changed from a pre-literate to a historical East Asian society. Developments within this society between the seventh and nineteenth centuries constitute the longest span of recorded Japanese history.

In the mid-nineteenth century, massive contacts with the West led to the rapid development of modern industries and the acceptance of new ideas and values. Japan transformed itself and became the first non-Western modern nation.

Within the long time span in which Japan developed its unique and brilliant variant of continental East Asian civilization, three periods must be further distinguished. First was the classical era of the Nara and Heian courts that extended from the seventh to the twelfth century. The second, the medieval period of rule by military houses, began in the thirteenth and continued into the sixteenth century. The third was the Tokugawa era, which extended from the early seventeenth to the mid-nineteenth century. During this last peaceful era, military houses still ruled but were incorporated within a framework of centralized government. Modern Japan, though brief in comparison, may be divided into two phases: the first, from the mid-nineteenth century to the end of World War II; the second, from 1945 to the present day.

This volume consists in the main of the Japan chapters of *The Heritage of World Civilization*, extensively revised and expanded. It provides a chronological framework and a narrative of Japan's history. It highlights periods of rule but also addresses social, economic, and cultural developments which were continuous and cut across rule-periods. There are, to be sure, excellent thick histories of Japan, particularly of the modern era. Their principal drawback is that length precludes the assignment of other readings. For the instructor who wishes to approach Japanese history topically or assign collections of original documents, monographs, novels and films, it is hoped that the brevity of this text will prove an advantage.

Brevity being the goal, the author asserts with seeming confidence many things that may be true only in the balance. Proper qualifications would take up many pages. Also, in telling the story of Japan's past the author has emphasized key historical variables, but in doing so has inevitably left out minor themes that merit attention. Reading assignments from the Suggested Readings at the end of each chapter may provide a counterpoint to the interpretations in the text.

Geography helps us to understand Japanese history. The climate varies widely, from the northern island of Hokkaido, where ice and snow may last into the spring, to the southern island of Kyushu, where palm trees dot the shores of Miyazaki and Kagoshima. But the central axis of the Japanese economy, culture, and polity has always been the temperate zone that stretches from western Honshu, through Osaka and Kyoto, to the Kanto plain and Tokyo in the east. Also of historical salience is the mountainous spine that runs through the length of the country and breaks up the country into regions. When central authority was weak, the regions often became politically autonomous. Maps identify most of the places mentioned in the text.

Even in studying the West—our own civilization—we catch only glimpses of what it meant, say, to be a merchant in late medieval Paris. What family, society, and nature looked like to a Japanese monk or merchant is yet more difficult to know. But some inkling may be gained from original sources. To this end, many translations of poems, philosophical essays, and passages from novels are included in the narrative and in boxed quotations. The immediacy of these writings provides windows onto the actual thought and feelings of actors in Japan's history. We find that Japanese living a thousand years ago had many of the same hopes, fears, joys, and sorrows that we do today. We recognize these shared feelings despite the powerful shaping of human experience by different cultural modalities and social institutions.

The final section of each chapter reviews chapter materials in a larger comparative context. The comparisons point out that similar processes occur in widely divergent societies. But it should be remembered that such similarities are always embedded in dense structures that are quite dissimilar. Each chapter is followed by review questions, which may help elucidate the main themes of the chapter.

Japanese names in the text are given in the Japanese fashion, with the family name first. Thus Itō Hirobumi is Mr. Itō, his given name, Hirobumi. Artists and writers, however, are often known by their "pen names." Natsume Sōseki, for example, was Natsume Kinnosuke as a youth, but later on, as an established novelist, was known as Natsume Sōseki or simply by his pen name as Sōseki. Japanese long vowels are indicated by a macron. Thus, Itō is pronounced I-toh, not Itō, and Sōseki as Soh-seki, not So-seki. Long vowels are omitted from familiar words treated as English terms. Ōsaka is just Osaka, Tokyo is Tokyo, and shōgun, except in the full Japanese title of *Seii Tai-Shōgun*, is just shogun.

In writing this book, I have drawn on many fine studies; my intellectual debts are legion and, as usual in a text of this nature, largely unacknowledged. But I would like to mention those to whom I owe a particular and personal debt, those whose ideas I have absorbed so completely as to think of as my own. Edwin O. Reischauer was first a mentor and then a colleague; Benjamin I. Schwartz was the colleague with whom I first taught a course on modern Japanese history; others with whom I have taught are Robert Bellah, Harold Bolitho, Peter Duus, Steve Ericson, Carol Gluck, Andrew Gordon, Howard Hibbett, Akira Iriye, Kate Nakai, Henry Rosovsky, Donald Shively, William Steele, and Ezra Vogel. I owe special thanks to my wife, Teruko Craig, who has tirelessly read and proofread the manuscript and made valuable suggestions. Finally, I would like to express my appreciation to the staff at Prentice Hall, to Judy Winthrop for her project management, and to Professor Chong-kun Yoon, who read the manuscript for the publisher and made numerous suggestions. All errors made are my own.

THE HERITAGE OF JAPANESE CIVILIZATION

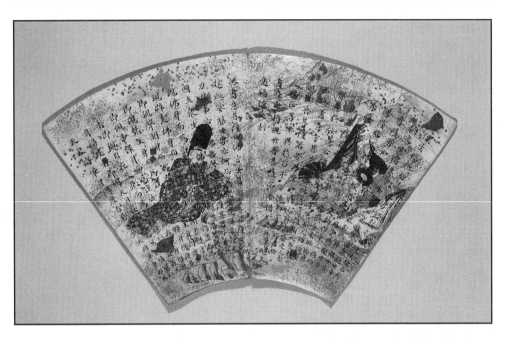

A twelfth century japanese fan. Superimposed on a painting of a gorgeously clad nobleman and his lady in a palace setting are verses in Chinese from a Buddhist sutra. The aesthetic pairing of sacred and secular was a feature of life at the Heian court. The fan could well have been used by a figure in Sei Shōnagon's *Pillow Book*. [Tokyo National Museum]

chapter one

Japanese History: Origins to the Twelfth Century

JAPANESE ORIGINS

Japanese hotly debate their origins. When a large Jōmon settlement was recently unearthed in Aomori Prefecture in the far north of Honshu, the discovery made the front page of newspapers throughout Japan. Bookstores have rows of books, most of them popular works, asking: Who are we and where did we come from? During the ice ages, Japan was connected by land bridges to Asia. Woolly mammoths entered the northern island of Hokkaido, and elephants, saber-toothed tigers, giant elks, and other continental fauna entered the lower islands. Did humans enter as well? Because Japan's acidic volcanic soil eats up bones, there are no early skeletal remains. The earliest evidence of human habitation is finely shaped stone tools dating from about 30,000 B.C.E. Then, from about 10,000 B.C.E., there is pottery, the oldest in the world, and from 8000 B.C.E., Jōmon or "cord-pattern" pottery.

Archaeologists are baffled by its appearance in an Old Stone Age hunting, gathering, and fishing society—when in all other early societies pottery developed along with agriculture as a part of New Stone Age culture. In addition to the elaborately decorated pots, archaeologists have also found marvelous figurines of animals and humans. Some of the latter, with slitted eyes like snow goggles, may depict female deities, but no one knows. During the Jōmon period, the food supply could support only a sparse population. Scholars estimate the late Jōmon population to have been about one quarter of a million, with the densest concentration on the Kanto plain in eastern Japan. Even today Jōmon pottery shards are sometimes found in Tokyo gardens.

THE YAYOI REVOLUTION

After 8000 years of Jōmon culture, a second phase of Japanese prehistory began about 300 B.C.E. It is called the Yayoi culture, after a place in Tokyo where its distinctive hard, pale-orange pottery was first unearthed. There is no greater break in the entire Japanese record than that between the Jōmon and the Yayoi. For at the beginning of the third century B.C.E., the bronze, iron, and agricultural revolutions—which in the Near East, India, and China had been separated by thousands of years

Along with the cord-patterned pots, the hunting and gathering Jōmon people produced mysterious figurines. Is this a female deity? Why are the eyes slitted like snow goggles? Earthenware with traces of pigment (Kamegoaka type); 24.8 cm high. [Asia Society, N.Y.: Mr. and Mrs. John D. Rockefeller 3rd Collection]

and each of which singly had wrought profound transformations—burst into Japan simultaneously.

The new technologies were brought to Japan by peoples moving across the Tsushima Straits from the Korean peninsula. It is uncertain whether these immigrants came as a trickle and were absorbed—the predominant view in Japan—or whether they came in sufficient numbers to push back the indigenous Jōmon people. Physical anthropologists say that skulls from early Yayoi sites in Kyushu and western Japan differ markedly from those of the Jōmon and are closer to the Japanese of

In 1972, Japanese archaeologists found this painting on the interior wall of a megalithic burial chamber at Takamatsuzuka in Nara Prefecture. The tomb dates to the 300–680 era and was covered with a mound of earth. The most sophisticated tomb painting found in Japan, it resembles paintings found in Korean and Chinese tombs. [Bildarchiv Preussischer Kulturbesitz]

today. But in eastern and northern Japan the picture is mixed, suggesting a mixture of the two peoples.

The Spread of the New Culture

The early Yayoi migrants, using the same seacraft by which they had crossed from Korea, spread along the coasts of northern Kyushu and western Honshu. Yayoi culture rapidly replaced Jōmon culture as far east in Japan as the present-day city of Nagoya. After that the Yayoi culture diffused overland into eastern Japan more slowly and with greater difficulty. In the east, climatic conditions were less favorable for agriculture, and a mixed agricultural-hunting economy lasted longer.

The early Yayoi "frontier settlements" were located next to their fields. Their agriculture was primitive: they scattered rice seed in swampy areas and used "slash-and-burn" techniques to clear uplands. By the first century C.E., the Yayoi population had so expanded that wars were fought for the best land. Excavations have found extensive stone-axe industries and skulls pierced by bronze and iron arrowheads. An early Chinese chronicle describes Japan as being made up of "more than one hundred countries" with wars and conflicts raging on all sides. During these wars villages were relocated to defensible positions on low hills away from the fields. From these wars emerged a more peaceful order of regional tribal states and a ruling class of aristocratic warriors. Late Yayoi excavations reveal villages once again situated alongside fields and far fewer stone axes.

During the third century C.E., a temporary hegemony was achieved over a number of such regional states by a queen named Pimiko. In the Chinese chronicle, Pimiko is described as a shaman who "occupied herself with magic and sorcery, bewitching the people." She was mature but unmarried.

> After she became the ruler, there were few who saw her. She had one thousand women as attendants but only one man. He served her food and drink and acted as a medium of communication. She resided in a palace surrounded by towers and stockades with armed guards in a state of constant vigilance.[1]

After Pimiko, references to Japan disappear from Chinese dynastic histories for a century and a half.

---

[1]L. C. Goodrich, ed., and R. Tsunoda, trans., *Japan in the Chinese Dynastic Histories* (South Pasadena, CA: Perkins Asiatic Monographs, 1951), p. 13.

Late Yayoi Japan as Presented in Chinese Histories

Weapons are spears, shields, swords, and wooden bows. The arrows are sometimes tipped with bone. The men all tattoo their faces and adorn their bodies with designs. The position and size of pattern indicate the difference of rank. The men's clothing is fastened breadth-wise and consists of one piece of cloth. The women tie their hair in bows, and their clothing, like our gown of one single piece of cloth, is put on by slipping it over the head. They use pink and scarlet to smear their bodies, as rice powder is used in China.

The women outnumber the men, and the men of importance have four or five spouses; the rest have two or three. The women are faithful and not jealous. There is no theft, and litigation is infrequent. When men break a law, their wives and children are confiscated; when the offense is serious, the offender's family is extirpated. At death mourning lasts for more than ten days, during which time members of the family weep and lament, without much drinking and eating, while their friends sing and dance.

When the lowly meet men of importance on the road, they stop and withdraw to the roadside. In conveying messages to them or addressing them, they either squat or kneel, with both hands on the ground. This is the way they show respect. When responding, they say "ah," which corresponds to the affirmative "yes."

When they go on voyages across the sea to visit China, they always select a man who does not arrange his hair, does not rid himself of fleas, lets his clothing [get as] dirty as it will, does not eat meat, and does not approach women. This man behaves like a mourner and is known as the fortune keeper. When the voyage turns out propitious, they all lavish on him slaves and other valuables. In case there is disease or mishap, they kill him, saying that he was not scrupulous in his duties.

L. C. Goodrich and R. Tsunoda, trans., *Japan in the Chinese Dynastic Histories* (South Pasadena, CA: Perkins Asiatic Monographs, © 1951), pp. 1, 2, 13, 11, respectively.

Tomb Culture and the Yamato State

Emerging directly from the Yayoi culture was an era, 300–600 C.E., characterized by giant tomb mounds, which even today dot the landscape of the Yamato plain in the Nara-Osaka region. Early tombs—patterned on those in Korea—were circular mounds of earth built atop megalithic burial chambers. Later tombs were sometimes keyhole-shaped. The tombs were surrounded by moats and adorned with clay cylinders and figures of warriors, horses, scribes, musicians, houses, boats, and the like. Early tombs, like the Yayoi graves that preceded them, contained mirrors, jewels, and other ceremonial objects. From the fifth century C.E., these objects were replaced by armor, swords, spears, and military trappings, reflecting a new wave of continental influences. The flow of people, culture, and technology from the Korean peninsula into Japan that began with Yayoi was continuous into historical times.

Japan reappeared in the Chinese chronicles in the fifth century C.E. This period was also covered in the earliest surviving Japanese accounts of their own history, *Records of Ancient Matters (Kojiki)* and *Records of Japan (Nihongi)* compiled in 712 and 720. The picture that emerges is of regional aristocracies under the loose hegemony of the Yamato "great kings." Historians use the geographic label "Yamato" because the courts of the great kings were located on the Yamato plain, the richest agricultural region of ancient Japan. The Yamato rulers also held lands and granaries throughout Japan. The tomb of the great king Nintoku, if it is his, is 486 meters long and 36 meters high, with twice the volume of the Great Pyramid of Egypt. By the fifth century C.E., the great kings possessed sufficient authority to commandeer laborers for such a project.

The great kings awarded Korean-type titles to court and regional aristocrats, titles that implied a national hierarchy centering on the Yamato court. That regional rulers had the same kind of political authority over their populations can be seen in the spread of tomb mounds throughout Japan.

The basic social unit of Yamato aristocratic society was the extended family *(uji)*, closer in size to a Scottish clan than to a modern household. Attached to these aristocratic families were groups of specialist workers called *be*. This word is of Korean origin and was originally used to designate potters, scribes, or others with special skills who had immigrated from Korea. It was then extended to include similar groups of indigenous workers and groups of peasants. Yamato society had a small class of slaves, possibly captured in wars. Many peasants were neither slaves nor members of specialized workers' groups.

What little is known of Yamato politics suggests that the court was the scene of incessant struggles for power between aristocratic families. There were also continuing efforts by the court to control outlying regions. Although marriage alliances were established and titles awarded, rebellions were not infrequent during the fifth and sixth centuries. Finally, there were constant wars with "barbarian tribes" in southern Kyushu and northeastern Honshu on the frontiers of "civilized" Japan.

The Yamato Court and Korea

During the era of the Yamato court, a three-cornered military balance developed on the Korean peninsula among the states of Paekche in the southwest, Silla in the east, and Koguryo in the north (see Map 1-1). Japan was an ally of Paekche and maintained extensive trade and military relations with a weak southern federation known as the Kaya States.

The Paekche connection enabled the Yamato court to expand its power within Japan. Imports of iron weapons and tools gave it military strength. The migration to Japan

Map 1-1   Yamato Japan ad Korea (ca. 500 C.E.).   Paekche was Japan's ally on the Korean peninsula. Silla, Japan's enemy, was the state that would eventually unify Korea. (Note: Nara was founded in 710; Heian in 794.)

of Korean potters, weavers, scribes, metal workers, and other artisans increased its wealth and influence. The great cultural significance of these immigrants can be gauged by the fact that many became established as noble families. Paekche also served as a conduit for the first elements of Chinese culture to reach Japan. Chinese writing was adopted for the transcription of Japanese names during the fifth or sixth century. Confucianism entered in 513, when Paekche sent a "scholar of the Five Classics." Buddhism arrived in 538, when a Paekche king sent a Buddha image, sutras, and possibly a priest.

Eventually the political balance on the peninsula led to a rupture in its relations with Japan. In 532 Paekche turned against Japan and joined Silla in attacking the Kaya States. By 562 the Kaya federation had been gobbled up. But the rupture of ties with Korea was less of a loss than it would have been earlier, for by this time Japan had established direct relations with China.

Religion in Early Japan

The indigenous religion of Yamato Japan was an animistic worship of the forces of nature, later given the name of *Shintō*, or "the way of the gods," to distinguish it from the newly arrived religion of Buddhism. Shinto probably entered Japan from the continent as a part of Yayoi culture. The underlying forces of nature might be embodied in a waterfall, a twisted tree, a strangely shaped boulder, a mountain, or a great leader who would be worshiped as a deity after his death. Mount Fuji was holy not as the abode of a god but because the mountain itself was an upwelling of a vital natural force. Even today in Japan, a gnarled tree trunk may be girdled with a straw rope and set aside as an object of veneration. The more potent forces of nature such as the sea, sun, wind, thunder, and lightning became personified as deities. The sensitivity to nature and natural beauty that pervades Japanese art and poetry probably owes much to Shinto.

Throughout Japan's premodern history most villages had shamans—religious specialists who, by entering a trance, could contact directly the inner forces of nature and gain the power to foretell the future or heal sickness. The queen Pimiko was such a shaman. The sorceress is also a stock figure in tales of ancient or medieval Japan. More often than not, women, receiving the command of a god, have founded the "new" religions in this tradition, even into the 19th and 20th centuries.

A second aspect of early Shinto was its connection with the state and the ruling posttribal aristocracy. Each aristocratic clan possessed a genealogy tracing its descent from a nature deity *(kami)* that it claimed as its original ancestor. A genealogy was a patent of nobility and a title to political authority. The head of a clan, also its chief priest, made sacrifices to its deity. When Japan was unified by the Yamato court, the myths of the leading clans were joined into a composite national myth. The deity of the Yamato great kings was the sun goddess, so she became the chief deity, while other gods assumed

Darkness and the Cave of High Heaven

The younger of the sun goddess was a mischief maker. Eventually the gods drove him out of heaven. On one occasion, he knocked a hole in the roof of a weaving hall and dropped in a dappled pony that he had skinned alive. One weaving maiden was so startled that she struck her genitals with the shuttle she was using and died.

What does this myth suggest regarding the social relations of the Shinto gods? Entering a cave and then reemerging signifies death and rebirth in the religions of many peoples, but here they may be different.

The Sun Goddess, terrified at the sight, opened the door of the heavenly rock cave, and hid herself inside. Then the Plain of High Heaven was shrouded in darkness, as was the Central Land of Reed Plains [Japan]. An endless night prevailed. The cries of the myriad gods were like the buzzing of summer flies, and myriad calamities arose.

The eight hundred myriad gods assembled in the bed of the Quiet River of Heaven. They asked one god to think of a plan. They assembled the long-singing birds of eternal night and made them sing. They took hard rocks from the bed of the river and iron from the Heavenly Metal Mountain and called in a smith to make a mirror. They asked the Jewel Ancestor God to make a string of 500 carved jewels eight feet long. They asked other gods to remove the shoulder blade of a male deer and to obtain cherry wood from Mount Kagu, and to perform a divination. They uprooted a sacred tree, attached the string of curved jewels to its upper branches, hung the large mirror from its middle branches, and sus-

lesser positions appropriate to the status of their clan. Had another clan won the struggle, its deity might have become paramount—perhaps a thunder god as in ancient Greece.

The *Records of Ancient Matters* and *Records of Japan* tell of the creation of Japan, of the deeds and misdeeds of gods on the "plain of high heaven," and of their occasional adventures on earth or in the underworld. In mid-volume, the stories of the gods, interspersed with genealogies of noble families, give way to stories of early great kings and early history. These kings, and later emperors descended from them, were viewed as the lineal descendants of the sun goddess and as "living gods." The Great Shrine of the sun goddess at Ise, accordingly, has always been the most important in Japan.

NARA AND HEIAN JAPAN

The second major turning point in Japanese history was its adoption of the higher civilization of China. This is a prime example of the worldwide process by which early

pended offerings of white and blue cloth from its lower branches.

One god held these objects as grand offerings and another intoned sacred words. The Heavenly Hand-Strong-Male God stood hidden beside the door. A goddess bound up her sleeves with club-moss from Mount Kagu, made a herb band from the spindle-tree, and bound together leaves of bamboo-grass to hold in her hands. Then she placed a wooden box facedown before the rock cave, stamped on it until it resounded, and, as if possessed, she exposed her breasts and pushed her shirt-band down to her genitals. The Plain of High Heaven shook as the myriad gods broke into laughter.

The Sun Goddess, thinking this strange, opened slightly the rock-cave door and said from within: "Since I have hidden myself I thought that the Plain of Heaven and the Central Land of the Reed Plains would all be in darkness. Why is it that the goddess makes merry and the myriad gods all laugh?"

The goddess replied: "We rejoice and are glad because there is here a god greater than you." While she spoke two other gods brought out the mirror and held it up before the Sun Goddess.

The Sun Goddess, thinking this stranger and stranger, came out the door and peered into the mirror. Then the Hand-Strong-Male God seized her hand and pulled her out. Another god drew a rope behind her and said: "You may not go back further than this."

So when the Sun Goddess had come forth, the Plain of High Heaven and the Central Land of the Reed Plains once again naturally shone in brightness.

From the *Records of Ancient Matters (Kojiki)*, translated by Albert Craig, with appreciation to Basil Hall Chamberlain and Donald L. Phillippi.

Chronology of Early Japanese History
8000–300 B.C.E.   Jōmon culture

Early Continental Influences
300 B.C.E.–300 C.E.	Yayoi culture
300–680 C.E.	Tomb culture and the Yamato state
680–850 C.E.	Chinese T'ang pattern in Nara and Early Heian Japan

---

"heartland civilizations" spread into their outlying areas. In Japan the process occurred between the 7th and 12th centuries and can best be understood in terms of three stages. The first stage was learning about China during the seventh century. The second stage, mostly during the eighth and early ninth centuries, saw the implantation in Japan of Chinese T'ang-type institutions. The third involved the transformation of these institutions to better fit them to conditions in Japan. By the 11th century the creative reworking of Chinese elements had led to a distinctive and often brilliant Japanese culture, unlike that of China or that of the earlier Yamato court.

Seventh Century

Historians once stressed the roles played by Prince Shōtoku (574–622) and Fujiwara no Kamatari (614–669) in adopting Chinese institutions. More recently, these early 7th century figures have been seen as important transmitters of Chinese ideas, but the institutions began later with the Emperor Temmu in the 680s.

Occasional embassies had been sent to China for some time, but regular embassies were begun by Shōtoku in 607. The embassies included traders, students, and Buddhist monks, as well as the representatives of the Yamato great kings. Japanese who studied in China played key roles in their own government when they returned home—like Third World students who study abroad today. They brought back a quickening flow of technology, art, Buddhist texts, and knowledge of Chinese legal and governmental systems. Shōtoku adopted the Chinese calendar and actively propagated Buddhism and Chinese notions of government.

Like Shōtoku, Fujiwara no Kamatari came to power as a result of factional struggles between powerful clans (or *uji*) at the court. Beginning in the Taika "year period," which started in 645, he initiated the so-called "Taika reforms." Many of these, like his new law codes, existed only on paper, but they moved Japanese thinking in a Chinese direction. The difficulties faced by preliterate Yamato Japanese in learning Chinese and in comprehending China's historical and philosophical culture were enormous.

Large-scale institutional changes using the T'ang model were begun by the Emperor Temmu (r. 672–686) and continued by his wife, the Empress Jitō (r. 686–692). Temmu's life illustrates the interplay between clan struggles at court and the adoption of Chinese institutions. He came to the throne by leading an alliance of eastern clans in rebellion against the previous great king, his nephew. The *Records of Japan* describe Temmu as "walking like a tiger through the eastern lands." He then used Chinese systems to consolidate his power. He promulgated a Chinese-type law code that greatly augmented the powers of the ruler. He styled himself as the "heavenly emperor" *(tennō)*, which thereafter replaced the earlier title of "great king." He rewarded his supporters with new court ranks and with positions in a new court government, both patterned after the T'ang example. He extended the authority of the court and increased its revenues by a survey of agricultural lands and a census of their population. In short, although the admiration for things Chinese must have been enormous, much of the borrowing was dictated by specific, immediate, and practical Japanese concerns.

Unlike the full-bodied T'ang ideal, this *bodhisattva* from the pre-Nara Hōryūji Temple reflects the artistic influence of the earlier Northern Wei dynasty. The T'ang style entered Japan during the Nara and early Heian periods. [Tokyo National Museum]

Nara and Early Heian Court Government

Until the eighth century the capital was usually moved each time an emperor died. In 710 a new capital, intended to be permanent, was established at Nara. It was laid out on a checkerboard grid like the Chinese capital at Ch'ang-an. But then it was moved again—some say to escape the meddling in politics of powerful Buddhist temples. A final move occurred in 794 to Heian (later Kyoto) on the plain north of Nara. This site remained the capital until the move to Tokyo in 1869. Even today, Kyoto's regular geometry reflects Chinese city planning.

The superimposition of a Chinese-type capital on a still-backward Japan produced as stark a contrast as any in history. In the villages, peasants—who worshiped the forces in mountains and trees—lived in pit dwellings and either planted in crude paddy fields or used slash-and-burn techniques of dry-land farming. In the capital stood pillared palaces in which dwelt the emperor and nobles, descended from the gods on high. They drank wine, wore silk, composed poetry, and enjoyed the paintings, perfumes, and pottery of the T'ang. Clustered about the capital were Buddhist temples, more numerous than in Nara, with soaring pagodas and sweeping tile roofs. With what awe must a peasant have viewed the city and its inhabitants!

The emperors at the Nara and Heian courts were both Confucian rulers with the majesty accorded by Chinese law and Shinto rulers descended from the sun goddess. Protected by an aura of the sacred, their lineage was never usurped. All Japanese history constitutes a single dynasty, although not a few emperors were killed and replaced by other family members in succession struggles.

Beneath the emperor, the same modified Chinese pattern prevailed. Like the T'ang, Japan had a Council of State, but it was more powerful than that of China. It was the office from which leading clans manipulated the authority of an emperor, who often reigned but did not rule. Beneath this council were eight ministries—two more than in China. One of the extra ministries was a Secretariat, the other an Imperial Household Ministry. Size affected function: while T'ang China had a population of 60 million, Nara Japan had only 4 or 5 million. There were fewer people to govern in Japan; there were no significant external enemies; and much of local rule, in the Yamato tradition, was in the hands of local clans. Consequently, more of the business of court government was with the court itself. Of the 6000 persons in the central ministries, more than 4000 were concerned in one way or another with the care of the imperial house. The Imperial Household Ministry, for example, had an official staff of 1296, whereas the Treasury had only 305 and Military Affairs only 198.

Under the central court government were 60-odd provinces, which were further subdivided into districts and villages. In pre-Nara times the regions had been governed by largely autonomous regional clans; but under the new system provincial governors were sent out from the capital. The new system reduced the old regional aristocrats to the lesser posts of district magistrates. The new system substantially increased the power of the central aristocracy.

In other respects, too, Japanese court government was unlike that of China. There were no eunuchs. There was little tension between emperor and bureaucracy—the main struggles were between clans. The T'ang shift from aristocracy toward an examination-based meritocracy was also absent in Japan. Apart from clerks and monastics, only aristocrats were educated, and only they were appointed to important official posts. Family counted more than schooling. A feeble attempt to establish an examination-based meritocracy failed completely.

Land and Taxes

The last Japanese embassy to China was in 839. By that time the zealous borrowing of Chinese culture had already slowed; the Japanese had taken in all they needed—or, perhaps, all they could handle—and were sufficiently self-confident to use Chinese ideas in innovative and flexible ways. The 350 years that followed until the end of the 12th century were a time of assimilation and evolutionary change. Nowhere was this more evident than in the system of taxation.

The land system of Nara and early Heian Japan was modeled on the equal field system of the early T'ang. All land belonged to the emperor; it was, in theory at least, redistributed every six years, and taxes were levied on the cultivators, not on the land. Those receiving land were liable for three taxes: a light tax in grain, a light tax on local products such as cloth or fish, and a heavy labor tax. The system was complex, requiring land surveys, the redrawing of boundaries, and elaborate land and population registers. Even in China, despite its sophisticated bureaucracy, the system broke down. In Japan the marvel is that this could be carried out at all. The evidence of old registers and recent aerial photographs suggests that it was, at least in western Japan. Its implementation speaks of the immense energy and ability of the early Japanese, who so quickly absorbed much of Chinese administrative techniques.

The equal field system broke down early. Whenever change in a society is imposed from above, the results tend to be uniform, but when changes occur willy-nilly within a social system, the results are messy and difficult to comprehend. The changes in taxes and land during the Heian period were of the latter type. Yet they are of such importance that an attempt must be made to describe them.

One big change was the rise of tax quotas payable in grain. First, officials discovered that peasants neglected land they did not own; so they abolished the redistribution of land and holdings became hereditary. Second, they noticed that tax labor was unskilled and performed with little enthusiasm, so they converted the labor tax into a grain tax and used the grain to pay laborers for their services. Third, they found themselves unable to maintain the elaborate population and land registers, so they simply gave each governor a quota of tax rice to send to the court, and each governor in turn gave quotas to the district magistrates in his province. They kept anything collected over the quota. In time the magistrates and the local notables and the miliary families associated with them used their share of the surplus to transform themselves into a new local military class.

A second important development, affecting about half of the land, was the conversion of tax-paying lands to tax-free estates known as *shōen*. Nobles and powerful temples used their influence at the court to obtain *immunities*—exemptions from taxation for their lands. From the ninth century, many small cultivators commended their holdings to such nobles, judging that they would be better off as serfs on tax-free estates than as free farmers subject to rapacious governors and magistrates. Since the pattern of commendation was random, the typical estate in Japan was composed of scattered parcels of land, unlike the unified estates of medieval Europe. The estates were managed for their noble owners by stewards appointed from among local notables. The stewards collected and sent to Kyoto the owner's portion of the harvest, and kept a small share for themselves. Like magistrates who collected tax-rice to fill quotas, the stewards had a vital interest in upholding the local order.

Rise of the Samurai

During the Nara period the court followed the Chinese model and conscripted about a third of able-bodied men between the ages of 21 and 60. The conscript army, however, proved inefficient, so in 792, two years before the start of the Heian period, the court decided to rely on local mounted warriors. In return for military service, the court remitted the warriors' taxes. Some were stationed in the capital and others in provinces. The Japanese verb "to serve" is *samurau*, so those who served became *samurai*—the noun form of the verb. Then, from the mid-Heian period, the officially recruited bands of local warriors were replaced by unofficial private bands. They constituted the military of Japan for the next half-millennium or so, until the emergence of foot-soldiers in the 15th and 16th centuries.

Being a samurai was expensive. Horses, armor, and weapons were costly and their use required long training. The primary weapon was the bow and arrow, used from the saddle. Those who could afford to be samurai were, in the main, from the families of magistrates, estate stewards, and local notables. They formed local bands to preserve law and order and, on occasion, to help collect taxes. At times local bands clashed. Late 9th century accounts tell of magistrates leading local forces against those of provincial governors, doubtless in connection with disputes over quota rice. Some samurai, as estate stewards, had ties with court nobles. Such ties led to the reliance on local private bands of mounted warriors during the second half of the Heian period.

From the early tenth century regional military bands began to form. They first broke into history in 935–940, when a regional military leader, a descendant of an emperor, became involved in a tax dispute. He captured several provinces, called himself the new emperor, and appointed a government of civil and military officials. The Kyoto court responded by recruiting another military band as its champion. The rebellion was quelled, and the rebel leader killed in battle. That the Kyoto court could summon a military band points out the connections that enabled it to maintain its political control of Japan. Many of these connections were to the local overseers of their extensive estates.

The rebellion was the first of a number of conflicts between regional military bands. Many wars were fought in eastern Japan—the "wild east" of those days. The east was more militarized because it was the headquarters for the periodic campaigns against the tribal peoples of the north. By the middle of the 12th century, local and regional military bands were in every part of Japan.

Late Heian Court Government

Even during the Nara period much of the elaborate apparatus of Chinese government was of little use. By the early Heian period the actual functions of government had been taken over by three new offices outside the Chinese system:

Audit officers. A newly appointed provincial governor had to report on the accounts of his predecessor. Agreement was rare. So from the end of the Nara period audit officers were sent to examine the books. By early Heian times these auditors had come to superintend the collection of taxes and most other capital–province relationships. They tried to halt the erosion of tax revenues, but as the quota and estate systems developed, this office had less and less to do.

Bureau of archivists. This bureau was established in 810 to record and preserve imperial decrees. Eventually it took over the executive function at the Heian court, drafting imperial decrees and attending to all aspects of the emperor's life.

Police commissioners. Established in the second decade of the ninth century to enforce laws and prosecute criminals, the commissioners eventually became responsible for all law and order in the capital. They absorbed military functions as well as those of the Ministry of Justice and the Bureau of Impeachment.

While these new institutions were evolving, shifts occurred in the control of the court.

1. The key figure remained the emperor, who had the power of appointments. Until the early Heian—say, the mid-ninth century—some emperors actually ruled or, more often, shared power with nobles of leading clans.

2. From 856 the northern branch of the Fujiwara clan became preeminent, and from 986 to 1086 its stranglehold on the court was absolute. The administrative offices of the Fujiwara house were almost more powerful than those of the central government, and the Fujiwara family monopolized all key government posts. They controlled the court by marrying their daughters to the emperor, forcing the emperor to retire after a son was born, and then ruling as regents for the new infant emperor. At times they even ruled as regents for adult emperors. Fujiwara Michinaga's words were no empty boast when he said, "As for this world, I think it is mine, nor is there a flaw in the full moon."

3. Fujiwara rule gave way, during the second half of the 11th century, to rule by retired emperors. The imperial family and lesser noble houses had long resented Fujiwara domination. Disputes within the Fujiwara house itself eventually enabled an emperor to regain control. Imperial control of government was reasserted by Emperor Shirakawa, who reigned from 1072 to 1086 and, abdicating at the age of 33, ruled for 43 years as retired emperor. After his death, another retired emperor continued in the same pattern until 1156.

   Retired Emperor Shirakawa set up offices in his quarters not unlike the administrative offices of the Fujiwara family. He employed talented nobles of lesser families and sought to reduce the number of tax-free estates by confiscating those of the Fujiwara. He failed in this attempt and instead garnered huge new estates for his own family. He developed strong ties to regional military leaders. His sense of his own power was reflected in his words—more a lament than a boast: "The only things that do not submit to my will are the waters of the Kamo River, the roll of the dice, and the soldier-monks [of the Tendai temple on Mount Hiei to the northeast of Kyoto]." But Shirakawa's powers were exercised in a capital city that was increasingly isolated from the changes in outlying regions, and even the city itself was plagued by fires, banditry, and a sense of impending catastrophe.

4. A momentous change occurred in 1156. The death of the ruling retired emperor precipitated a struggle for power between another retired emperor and the reigning emperor. Each called on a powerful Fujiwara and a regional military force for backing. The military force led by Taira Kiyomori defeated that led by a Minamoto, though it was challenged again in the Heiji War of 1159–1160. Taira Kiyomori had come to Kyoto to uphold an emperor, but finding himself in charge, he stayed to rule. His pattern of rule was quite Japanese: court nobles kept their court offices; the reigning emperor, who had been supported by Kiyomori, retired and took control of the offices of the retired emperor and of the estates of the imperial family; the head of the Fujiwara family kept the post of regent, while Taira Kiyomori married his daughter to the new emperor, and when a son was born Kiyomori forced the emperor to retire and ruled as the maternal grandfather of the infant emperor. That is to say, the Taira ruled as a new stratum atop the old court heirarchy.

Who Was in Charge at the Nara and Heian Courts	
710–856	Emperors or combinations of nobles
856–1086	Fujiwara nobles
1086–1160	Retired emperors
1160–1180	Military house of Taira

ARISTOCRATIC CULTURE AND BUDDHISM IN NARA AND HEIAN JAPAN

If the parts of a culture could be put on a scale and weighed like sugar or flour, we would conclude that the culture of Nara and early Heian Japan was overwhelmingly one of Shinto religious practices and village folkways, an extension of the culture of the late Yamato period. The early Heian aristocracy was small—one tenth of one percent of Japan's population—and was encapsulated in the routines of court life, as were Buddhist monks in the rounds of their monastic life. Most of the court

In the Heiji War of 1159–1160, regional samurai bands became involved in Kyoto court politics. This is a scroll painting of the burning of the Sanjō Palace. Handscroll; ink and colors on paper, 41.3 × 699.7 cm. [Courtesy of Boston. Fenollosa-Weld Collection Museum of Fine Arts,]

Aristocratic Taste at the Fujiwara Court: Sei Shōnagon Records Her Likes and Dislikes

Here are some passages from Sei Shōnagon's the *Pillow Book*, one of the masterpieces of Heian Japan.

In what sense can a literary work such as this also be considered a historical document? What kind of information can it provide about court life?

Elegant Things

A white coat worn over a violet waistcoat.
Duck eggs.
Shaved ice mixed with liana syrup and put in a new silver bowl.
A rosary of rock crystal.
Snow on wistaria or plum blossoms.
A pretty child eating strawberries.

Features That I Particularly Like

Someone has torn up a letter and thrown it away. Picking up the pieces, one finds that many of them can be fitted together.

A person in whose company one feels awkward asks one to supply the opening or closing line of a poem. If one happens to recall it, one is very pleased. Yet often on such occasions one completely forgets something that one would normally know.

Entering the Empress's room and finding that ladies-in-waiting are crowded round her in a tight group, I go next to a pillar which is some distance from where she is sitting. What a delight it is when Her Majesty summons me to her side so that all the others have to make way!

Hateful Things

A lover who is leaving at dawn announces that he has to find his fan and his paper. "I know I put them somewhere last night," he says. Since it is pitch dark, he gropes about the room, bumping into the furniture and muttering, "Strange! Where on earth can they be?" Finally he discovers the objects. He thrusts the paper into the breast of his robe with a great rustling sound; then he snaps open his fan and busily fans away with it. Only now is he ready to take his leave. What charmless behavior! "Hateful" is an understatement.

A good lover will behave as elegantly at dawn as at any other time. He drags himself out of bed with a look of dismay on his face. The lady urges him on: "Come, my friend, it's getting light. You don't want anyone to find you here." He gives a deep sigh, as if to say that the night has not been nearly long enough and that it is agony to leave. Once up, he does not instantly pull on his trousers. Instead he comes close to the lady and whis-

culture had only recently been imported from China. There had not been time for commoners to ape their betters or for the powerful force of the indigenous culture to reshape that of the elite.

The resulting cultural gap helps to explain why the aristocrats, insofar as we can tell from literature, found the commoners to be odd, incomprehensible, indeed, hardly human. The writings of the courtiers reflect little sympathy for the suffering

pers whatever was left unsaid during the night. Even when he is dressed, he still lingers, vaguely pretending to be fastening his sash.

Presently he raises the lattice, and the two lovers stand together by the side door while he tells her how he dreads the coming day, which will keep them apart; then he slips away. The lady watches him go, and this moment of parting will remain among her most charming memories.

In Spring It Is the Dawn

In spring it is the dawn that is most beautiful. As the light creeps over the hills, their outlines are dyed a faint red and wisps of purplish cloud trail over them.

In summer the nights. Not only when the moon shines, but on dark nights too, as the fireflies lit to and fro, and even when it rains, how beautiful it is!

In autumn the evenings, when the glittering sun sinks close to the edge of the hills and the crows fly back to their nests in threes and fours and twos; more charming still is a file of wild geese, like specks in the distant sky. When the sun has set, one's heart is moved by the sound of the wind and the hum of the insects.

In winter the early mornings. It is beautiful indeed when snow has fallen during the night, but splendid too when the ground is white with frost; or even when there is no snow or frost, but it is simply very cold and the attendants hurry from room to room stirring up the fires and bringing charcoal, how well this fits the season's mood! But as noon approaches and the cold wears off, no one bothers to keep the braziers alight, and soon nothing remains but piles of white ashes.

Things That Have Lost Their Power

A large tree that has been blown down in a gale and lies on its side with its roots in the air.

The retreating figure of a sumo wrestler who has been defeated in a match.

A woman, who is angry with her husband about some trifling matter, leaves home and goes somewhere to hide. She is certain that he will rush about looking for her; but he does nothing of the kind and shows the most infuriating indifference. Since she cannot stay away for ever, she swallows her pride and returns.

and hardships of the people—except in Chinese-style poetry, where such feelings were required. When the fictional Prince Genji stoops to an affair with an impoverished woman, she inevitably turns out to be a princess. Sei Shōnagon was not atypical as a writer: she was offended by the vulgarity of mendicant nuns; laughed at an illiterate old man whose house had burned down; and finds lacking in charm the eating habits of carpenters, who wolfed down their food a bowl at a time.

Heian high culture resembled a hothouse plant. It was protected by the political influence of the court. It was nourished by the flow of tax revenues and income from estates. Under these conditions, the aristocrats of the never-never land of Prince Genji indulged in a unique way of life and created canons of elegance and taste that are striking even today. The speed with which T'ang culture was assimilated and reworked was amazing. A few centuries after Mediterranean culture had been introduced into northern Europe, there appeared nothing even remotely comparable to Lady Murasaki's *Tale of Genji* or Sei Shōnagon's *Pillow Book*.

Chinese Tradition in Japan

Education at the Nara and Heian courts was largely a matter of reading Chinese books and acquiring the skills needed to compose poetry and prose in Chinese. These were daunting tasks, not only because there was no prior tradition of scholarship in Japan but also because the two languages were so dissimilar. To master written Chinese and use it for everyday written communications was as great a challenge for the Nara Japanese as it would have been for any European of the same century. But the challenge was met. From the Nara period until the 19th century, most philosophical and legal writings and the majority of the histories, essays, and religious texts in Japan were written in Chinese. From a Chinese perspective the writings may leave something to be desired. It would be astonishing if this were not the case, for the soul of language is the music of the spoken tongue. But the Japanese writers were competent, and the feelings they expressed were authentic—when not copybook exercises in the style of a Chinese master. In 883, when the courtier Sugawara Michizane wrote a poem on the death of his son, he quite naturally wrote it in Chinese. The poem began

> Since Amaro died I cannot sleep at night;
> if I do, I meet him in dreams and tears come coursing down.
> Last summer he was over three feet tall;
> this year he would have been seven years old.
> He was diligent and wanted to know how to be a good son,
> Read his books and recited by heart the "Poem on the Capital." [2]

The capital was Ch'ang-an; the poem was one "used in Japan by all little boys learning to read Chinese."

Not only were Japanese writings in Chinese a vital part of the Japanese cultural tradition, but the original Chinese works were, too. The T'ang poet Po Chü-i was early appreciated and widely read; later, Tu Fu and Li Po were also read and admired. Chinese

---

[2]H. Sato and B. Watson, trans., *From the Country of Eight Islands* (Seattle: University of Washington Press, 1981), p. 121.

The Development of Japanese Writing

No two languages could be more different than Chinese and Japanese. Chinese is non-syllabic, uninflected, and tonal. Japanese is polysyllabic, highly inflected, and atonal. To adopt Chinese writing for use in Japanese was thus no easy task. What the Japanese did at first—when they were not simply learning to write in Chinese—was to use certain Chinese ideographs as a phonetic script. For example, in the Man'yōshū, the eight-century poetic anthology, *shira-nami* (white wave) was written with 之 for *shi*, 良 for *ra*, 奈 for *na*, and 美 *mi*. Over several centuries, these phonetic ideographs evolved into a uniquely Japanese phonetic script:

	Original Chinese Ideograph	Simplified Ideograph	Phonetic Script (*kana*)
shi	之	?	し
ra	良	方	ら
na	奈	京	な
mi	美	彡	ケ

It is apparent in the above examples how the original ideograph was first simplified according to the rules of calligraphy and was then further simplified into a phonetic script known as *kana*. In modern Japanese, Chinese ideographs are used for nouns and verb stems, and the phonetic script is used for inflections and particles.

学生は図書館へ行きました。

Students/as for/library/to/went.
(The students went to the library.)

In the above sentence, the Chinese ideographs are the forms with many strokes, and the phonetic script is shown in the simpler, cursive forms.

history was read, and its stock figures were among the heroes and villains of the Japanese historical consciousness. Chinese history became the mirror in which Japan saw itself, despite the differences in their societies. Buddhist stories and the Confucian canon also became Japanese classics, continuously accessible and consulted over the centuries for their wisdom and moral guidance. The parallel might be the acceptance of such "foreign books" as the Bible, Plato, and Aristotle in medieval and Renaissance England.

Birth of Japanese Literature

Stimulated by Chinese examples, and drawing on a tradition of songs, the Japanese began to compose poetry in their native tongue. The first great anthology was the *Collection of Ten Thousand Leaves (Man'yōshū)*, compiled in about 760. It contains 4516 poems. The poems are fresh, sometimes simple and straightforward, but often sophisticated. They reveal a deep sensitivity to nature and strong human relationships between husband and wife, parents and children. They also display a love for the land of Japan and links to a Shinto past.

An early obstacle to the development of a Japanese poetic tradition was the difficulty of transcribing Japanese sounds. In the *Ten Thousand Leaves*, Chinese characters were used as phonetic symbols. But there was no standardization, and the work soon became unintelligible. In 951, when an empress wished to read it, a committee of poets deciphered the work and put it into *kana*, the new syllabic script that had been devised a century earlier. A second important anthology was the *Collection of Ancient and Modern Times*, compiled in 905. It was written entirely in *kana*.

The invention of *kana* opened the gate to the most brilliant achievements of the Heian period. Most of the new works and certainly the greatest were by women, as most men were busy writing Chinese. One genre of writing was the diary or travel diary. An outstanding example was the *Izumi Shikibu Diary*, in which the court lady Izumi Shikibu reveals her tempestuous loves through a record of poetic exchanges.

The greatest works of the period were by Sei Shōnagon and Murasaki Shikibu. Both were daughters of provincial officials serving at the Heian court. The *Pillow Book* of Sei Shōnagon contains sharp, satirical, amusing essays and literary jottings that reveal the demanding aristocratic taste of the early 11th-century Heian court, where, as Sir George Sansom said, "religion became an art and art a religion." [3]

The *Tale of Genji*, written by Murasaki Shikibu in about 1010, was the world's first novel. Emerging out of a short tradition of lesser works in which prose was a setting for poetry, *Genji* is a work of sensitivity, originality, and acute psychological delineation of character. It tells of the life, loves, and sorrows of Prince Genji, the son of an imperial concubine, and, after his death, of his son Kaoru. The novel spans three quarters of a century and is historical in nature, although the court society it describes is more emperor-centered than was the Fujiwara age in which Murasaki lived. The book may be seen as having had a "definite and serious purpose." In one passage Genji twits a court lady whom he finds absorbed in reading an extravagant romance, "hardly able to lift her eyes from the book in front of her." But then Genji relents and says

> I think far better of this art than I have led you to suppose. Even its practical value is immense. Without it what should we know of how people lived in the past, from the Age of the Gods down to the present day? For

---

[3]G. Sansom, *Japan, A Short Cultural History* (New York: Appleton-Century-Crofts, 1962), p. 239.

history books such as the *Chronicles of Japan* show us only one small corner of life; whereas these diaries and romances, which I see piled around you contain, I am sure, the most minute information about all sorts of people's private affairs.[4]

Nara and Heian Buddhism

The Six Sects of the Nara period each represented a separate philosophical doctrine within Mahayana Buddhism, the type of Buddhism that had spread from India to China, Vietnam, and Korea. Their monks trained as religious specialists in monastic communities set apart from the larger society. They studied, read sutras, copied texts, meditated, and joined in rituals. The typical monastery was a self-contained community with a Golden Hall for worship, a pagoda that housed a relic or sutra, a belfry that rang the hours of the monastic regimen, a lecture hall, a refectory, and dormitories with monks' cells.

As in China, monasteries and temples were directly tied in with the state. Tax revenues were assigned for their support. In 741 the government established temples in every province. Monks reading sutras, it was felt, would protect the country. Monks prayed for the health of the emperor and for rain in time of drought. The Temple of the Healing Buddha (Yakushiji) was built by an emperor when his consort fell ill. In China, to protect tax revenues and the family, laws had been enacted to limit the number of monks and nuns. In Nara Japan, where Buddhism spread only slowly outside the capital area, the same laws took on a prescriptive force. The figure that had been a limit in China became a goal in Japan. Thus, the involvement of the state was patterned on that of China, but its role was far more supportive.

Japan in the seventh and eighth centuries was also much less culturally developed than China. The Japanese had come to Buddhism not from the philosophical perspectives of Confucianism or Taoism but from the magic and mystery of Shinto. The appeal of Buddhism to the early Japanese was, consequently, in its colorful and elaborate rituals; in the gods, demons, and angels of the Mahayana pantheon; and, above all, in the beauty of Buddhist art. The philosophy took longer to establish itself. The speed with which the Japanese mastered the construction of temples with elaborate wooden brackets and gracefully arching tile roofs, as well as the serene beauty of Nara Buddhist sculpture, wall paintings, and lacquer temple altars, was no less an achievement than their establishment of a political system based on the T'ang codes.

Japan's cultural identity was also different. In China Buddhism was always viewed as Indian and alien. Its earliest Buddha statues, like those of northwestern

[4]R. Tsunoda, W. T. de Bary, and D. Keene, eds., *Sources of the Japanese Tradition* (New York: Columbia University Press, 1958), p. 181.

India, looked Greek. That Buddhism was part of a non-Chinese culture was one factor leading to the Chinese persecution of Buddhists during the ninth century. In contrast, Japan's cultural identity or cultural self-consciousness took shape only during the Nara and early Heian periods. One element in that identity was the imperial cult derived from Shinto. But as a religion, Shinto was no match for Buddhism. The Japanese were aware that Buddhism was foreign, but it was no more so than Confucianism and all the rest of the T'ang culture that had helped reshape the Japanese identity, so there was no particular bias against it. As a result, Buddhism entered deeply into Japanese culture and retained its vitality longer. Not until the 17th or 18th centuries did a few Japanese scholars become so Confucian as to be anti-Buddhist.

In 794 the court moved to Heian. Buddhist temples soon became as entrenched in the new capital as they had been in Nara. The two great new Buddhist sects of the Heian era were Tendai and Shingon.

Saichō (766–822), the founder of the Tendai sect, had established a temple on Mount Hiei to the northwest of Kyoto in 785. He went to China as a student monk in 804 and returned the following year with the syncretic teachings of the Tendai sect. He spread the doctrine that salvation was not solely for monastic specialists but could be attained by all who led a life of contemplation and moral purity. He instituted strict monastic rules and a 12-year training curriculum for novice monks at his mountain monastery. Over the next few centuries, the sect grew until thousands of temples had been built on Mount Hiei, which remained a center of Japanese Buddhism until it was destroyed in the wars of the 16th century. Many later Japanese sects emerged from the Tendai fold, stressing one or another doctrine of its syncretic teachings.

The Shingon sect was begun by Kūkai (774–835). He studied Confucianism, Taoism, and Buddhism at the court university. Having decided that Buddhism was superior, he became a monk at the age of 18. In 804 he went to China with Saichō. He returned two years later bearing the Shingon doctrines and founded a monastery on Mount Kōya to the south of the Nara plain and far from the new capital. Kūkai was an extraordinary figure. He was a bridge builder, a poet, an artist, and one of the three great calligraphers of his age. He is sometimes credited with inventing the *kana* syllabary and with introducing tea into Japan. Shingon doctrines center on an eternal and cosmic Buddha, of whom all other Buddhas are manifestations. *Shingon* means "true word" or "mantra," a verbal formula with mystical powers. It is sometimes called *esoteric Buddhism* because it had secret teachings that were passed from master to disciple. In China Shingon had died out as a sect in the persecutions of the mid-ninth century, but it was tremendously successful in Japan. Its doctrines even spread to the Tendai center on Mount Hiei. Part of the appeal was in its air of mystery and its complex rituals involving signs, the manipulation of religious objects, and mandalas— maps of the cosmic Buddhist universe.

During the later Heian period, Buddhism began to be assimilated. At the village level, the folk religion of Shinto took in Buddhist elements. In the high culture of the capital, Shinto was almost absorbed by Buddhism. Shinto deities came to be seen as the local manifestations of universal Buddhas. The cosmic or "Great Sun Buddha" of the Shingon sect, for example, was easily identified with the sun goddess. Often, great Buddhist temples had smaller Shinto shrines on their grounds. The Buddha watched over Japan; the shrine deity guarded the temple itself. Not until the mid-19th century was Shinto disentangled from Buddhism, and then for political ends.

EARLY JAPANESE HISTORY IN HISTORICAL PERSPECTIVE

A fair question to ask of any civilization is how many historical (or prehistorical) layers it has and how each layer relates to the next. In Japan the first, the longest-lasting, and certainly the most deeply buried layer was Jōmon culture. Archaeologists have uncovered village sites, cemeteries, and kitchen middens and deduced a picture of material life in a hunting, fishing, and gathering society. Yet we know next to nothing of Jōmon culture, language, or spiritual life. Nor can we specify the Jōmon contributions to the era that followed, though doubtless there were some in northern Japanese villages.

The Yayoi layer is a wholly different story. In four key areas the Yayoi imprint remains indelible in subsequent Japanese civilization, though each underwent further transformations: the language of the Yayoi people became Japanese; their religion became Shinto; their agricultural settlements, while primitive, were the start of a village tradition that continued into the 20th century; and their leaders began the pattern of rule by aristocrats that continued to the 19th century.

The third historical layer, the Chinese culture of the Nara and early Heian eras and its distinctive Japanese development had so wide and deep an influence that to detail its contribution would require a recapitulation of Japanese history. Here we will merely point out that this Nara-Heian layer was geographically variable. In Kyoto (Heian) and the capital region of western Japan it was dense and rich. The *Tale of Genji* describes a way of life that was literate, sophisticated, and elegant—wholly unlike that of the countryside. In the provinces, despite government offices and temples, Nara-Heian high culture was thin. A court noble might welcome an appointment as a provincial governor as an opportunity to recoup his family for-tunes. But the price he paid was to live for several years in a society he viewed as rude and backward. Attempts were made to reproduce Heian culture in outlying areas—Hiraizumi in the far north comes to mind—but in general provincial contri-butions to Japan's higher culture were small during this era. In Aomori in northern-most Honshu, for instance, Hokkaido was not then a part of Japan), some pottery of the 12th century still resembled Jōmon ware. Travelling outward from the capital was travelling backward in time.

REVIEW QUESTIONS

1. Can we say that Yayoi society was shaped by its eastern frontier? What changes in this society led to the building of tombs and the emergence of the Yamato great kings?

2. Did borrowing from China fundamentally change Japan during the Nara and Heian periods? Did Japan fundamentally change what it borrowed?

3. Describe Buddhism in the Nara and Heian periods. How does it differ from Shinto? What accounts for its acceptance in Japan?

4. New systems of taxation and government evolved in mid-Heian Japan from institutions borrowed from T'ang China. Are there parallels in the way the Japanese literature of the period evolved?

SUGGESTED READINGS

M. Adolphson, *The Gates of Power: Monks, Courtiers, and Warriors in Premodern Japan* (2000). A new interpretation stressing the importance of temples in the political life of Heian and Kamakura Japan.

C. Blacker, *The Catalpa Bow* (1975). A fascinating and sympathetic study of contemporary folk Shinto, a religion with roots in ancient Japan.

R. Borgen, *Sugawara no Michizane and the Early Heian Court* (1986). A study of a famous courtier and poet.

D. Brown, ed., Vol. 1 of the *Cambridge History of Japan: Ancient Japan* (1993). A multi-author volume.

W. W. Farris, *Heavenly Warriors: The Evolution of Japan's Military, 500–1300* (1992). An in-depth study of the subject.

W. W. Farris, *Population, Disease, and Land in Early Japan, 645–900* (1985). An innovative reinterpretation of early history.

W. W. Farris, *Sacred Texts and Buried Treasures* (1998). Studies of Japan's prehistory and early history, based on recent Japanese research.

K. F. Friday, *Hired Swords: The Rise of Private Warrior Power in Early Japan* (1991). The interpretation in this book may be compared to that in Farris's *Heavenly Warriors*.

J. W. Hall, *Government and Local Power in Japan, 500–1700: A Study Based on Bizen Province* (1966). One of the finest books on Japanese history to 1700.

D. Keene, ed., *Anthology of Japanese Literature from the Earliest Era to the Mid-Nineteenth Century* (1955). A basic source for this and later periods.

M. Kitagawa, *Religion in Japanese History* (1966). A survey of religion in premodern Japan.

I. H. LEVY, *The Ten Thousand Leaves* (1981). A fine translation of Japan's earliest poetry collection.

I. MORRIS, trans., *The Pillow Book of Sei Shonagon* (1967). Incisive observations of Heian court life by the Jane Austen of Heian Japan.

S. MURASAKI, *The Tale of Genji*, trans. by E. G. Seidensticker (1976). A superb translation of the world's first novel and the greatest work of Japanese fiction.

S. MURASAKI, *The Tale of Genji*, trans. by A. Waley (1952). An earlier and freer translation. Compare it side by side with that of Seidensticker.

R. J. PEARSON et al., eds., *Windows on the Japanese Past: Studies in Archaeology and Prehistory* (1986).

L. PHILIPPI, trans., *Kojiki* (1968). Japan's ancient myths. The best translation despite the ideosyncratic romanizations of names.

J. N. RABINOVITCH, trans., *Shomonki, the Story of Masakado's Rebellion* (1986). The tale of Taira Masakado's rebellion against the Kyoto court in the tenth century.

E. O. REISCHAUER, *Ennin's Diary, the Record of a Pilgrimage to China in Search of the Law* and *Ennin's Travels in T'ang China* (1955).

E. O. REISCHAUER AND A. M. CRAIG, *Japan: Tradition and Transformation* (1989). A more detailed text covering the total sweep of Japanese history from the early beginnings through the 1980s.

R. TSUNODA, W. T. DE BARY, AND D. KEENE, comps., *Sources of the Japanese Tradition* (1958). A collection of original religious, political, and philosophical writings from each period of Japanese history. The best reader. A new expanded edition is forthcoming.

Construction of the "White Heron" castle in Himeji was begun during the Warring States era and was completed shortly after 1600. During the Tokugawa peace, it remained as a monument to the glory of the daimyo. Today it can be seen from the "bullet train." [Japan Airlines/Photo by Morris Simoncelli]

chapter two

Medieval Japan: The Twelfth to Sixteenth Centuries

CHAPTER OUTLINE

Kamakura and Ashikaga Japan
Buddhism and Medieval Culture
Warring States Era
Medieval Japan in Historical Perspective

KAMAKURA AND ASHIKAGA JAPAN

The late 12th century was another major turning point in Japanese history. It began the shift from centuries of rule by a civil aristocracy to centuries of rule by one that was military. It saw the formation of the *bakufu* (tent government), a completely non-Chinese type of government. It saw the emergence of the *shōgun* as the de facto ruler of Japan—though in theory he remained a military official of the emperor's government. Changes in society and family were set in motion. It marked the beginning of new cultural forms and initiated changes in family and social organization.

Rise of Minamoto Yoritomo

Taira Kiyomori's seizure of Kyoto in 1160 fell far short of being a national hegemony, for other military bands still flourished elsewhere in Japan. After Kiyomori's victory, the Taira embraced the elegant lifestyle of the Kyoto court while ties to their base area along the Inland Sea weakened. They assumed that their tutelage over the court would be as enduring as had been that of the Fujiwara. In the meantime, the Minamoto were rebuilding their strength in eastern Japan. In 1180 Minamoto Yoritomo (1147–1199) responded to a call to arms by a disaffected prince, seized control of eastern Japan (the rich Kanto Plain), and began the war that ended in 1185 with the downfall of the Taira.

Yoritomo's victory was national, for his armies had ranged over most of Japan. After his victory warriors from every area vied to become his vassals. Wary of the blandishments of Kyoto that had weakened the Taira forces, Yoritomo set up his headquarters at Kamakura, 30 miles south of present-day Tokyo, at the southern edge of his base of power in eastern Japan (see Map 2-1). He called his government the *bakufu* in contrast to the civil government in Kyoto. Like the house government of the Fujiwara, or the "cloister government" of the retired emperors, the offices he established were few and practical: one to deal with his samurai retainers, one to administer and execute his policies, and one to hear legal suits. Each office was staffed by vassals. The decisions of these offices, built up into a body of customary law, were codified in 1232 as the Jōei

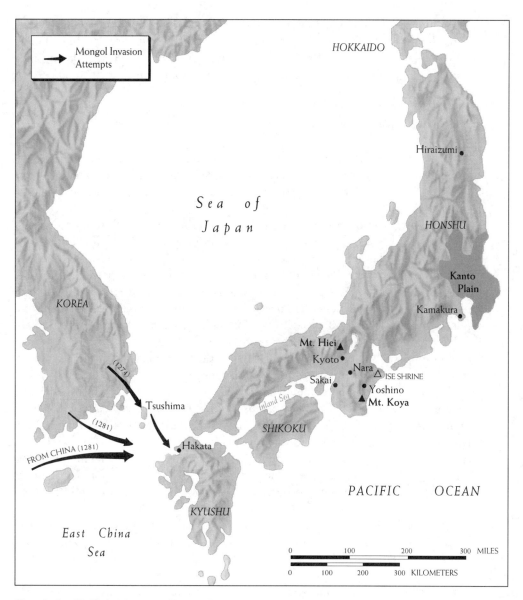

Map 2–1 Medieval Japan and the Mongol Invasions. The arrows show the routes of the invading Mongol armies. Kamakura, on the Kanto Plain, and Kyoto, in western Japan contended for power during the Kamakura period (1185–1333). The *bakufu* was at Kamakura and the court at Kyoto. After 1336 the Ashikaga *bakufu* established itself in Kyoto and absorbed the powers of the court.

Code. Yoritomo also appointed military governors in each province and military stewards on the former estates of the Taira and others who had fought against him. These appointments carried the right to some income from the land. The rest of the income, as earlier, went to Kyoto as taxes or as revenues to the noble owners of the estates.

The Question of Feudalism

Scholars often contend that Yoritomo's rule marks the start of feudalism in Japan. Feudalism may be defined in terms of three criteria: lord–vassal relationships, fiefs given in return for military service, and a warrior ethic. Do these apply to Kamakura Japan?

Certainly, the mounted warriors who made up the armies of Yoritomo were predominantly his vassals, not his kin. The Minamoto and Taira houses had originally been extended families, much like the Fujiwara or the earlier Yamato nobility. Yoritomo's brothers were among his generals. But after he came to power, he favored his vassals over his kin, and lateral blood ties gave way to the vertical and political lord–vassal bond. As for fiefs, the answer is ambiguous. Kamakura vassals received rights to income from land in exchange for military service. But the income was usually a slice of the surplus from the estates of Kyoto nonmilitary aristocrats. While a kind of property, such rights were not a fief in the usual meaning of the term. Fief as grants of land did not appear until the 15th century.

However, there is no ambiguity regarding the warrior ethic, which had been developing among regional military bands for several centuries before 1185. The samurai prized martial qualities such as bravery, cunning, physical strength, and endurance. They gave their swords names. Their sports were hunting, hawking, and archery —loosing their arrows at the target while riding at full tilt. If the military tales of the period are to be believed, combat was often individual, and before engaging in battle warriors called out their pedigrees. That is to say, samurai thought of themselves as a military aristocracy that practiced "the way of the bow and arrow," "the way of the warrior," and so on. In the Buddhist-tinged *Tale of Heike*, a military romance recounting the struggle between the Taira and the Minamoto, a Taira general asks a vassal from eastern Japan

> "Sanemori, in the eight eastern provinces are there many men who are as mighty archers as you are?"
>
> "Do you then consider me a mighty archer?" asked Sanemori with a scornful smile. "I can only draw an arrow thirteen handbreadths long. In the eastern provinces there are any number of warriors who can do so. There is one famed archer who never draws a shaft less than fifteen handbreadths long. So mighty is his bow that four or five ordinary men must

pull together to bend it. When he shoots, his arrow can easily pierce two or three suits of armor at once. Even a warrior from a small estate has at least five hundred soldiers. They are bold horsemen who never fall, nor do they let their horses stumble on the roughest road. When they fight, they do not care if even their parents or children are killed; they ride on over their bodies and continue the battle.

"The warriors of the western province are quite different. If their parents are killed, they retire from the battle and perform Buddhist rites to console the souls of the dead. Only after the mourning is over will they fight again. If their children are slain, their grief is so deep that they cease fighting altogether. When their rations have given out, they plant rice in the fields and go out to fight only after reaping it. They dislike the heat of summer. They grumble at the severe cold of winter. This is not the way of the soldiers of the eastern provinces." [1]

The Taira soldiers "heard his words and trembled."

The Kamakura military band thus pretty well fits our definition of feudalism. Nonetheless, qualifications are in order, as warrior bands were only one part of the whole society. One large qualification is that Kamakura Japan still had two political centers. The *bakufu* had military authority, but the Kyoto court continued the late Heian pattern of civil rule. It appointed civil governors; it received tax revenues; and it controlled the region about Kyoto. Noble families, retired emperors, and the great Buddhist temples—in control of vast estates—also contributed to Kyoto's ongoing power. It also remained the fount of rank and honors. After his victory in 1185, Yoritomo asked the emperor for the title of "barbarian-quelling generalis-simo" *(Sei i tai shōgun*, conventionally shortened to *shōgun*). He was refused, and only after the retired emperor died in 1192 did he get the title to match his power. Even then, the award of the title was justified only because Yoritomo was a Minamoto off-shoot of the imperial line.

The small size of Yoritomo's vassal band is an even more telling argument against viewing Japan as fully feudal at this time. Leading historians estimate that the number was about 2000 before 1221 and 3000 thereafter. Most vassals were con-centrated in eastern Japan. But even if as many as half of them were distributed about the rest of the country as military governors and stewards, there would have been only 100 in a region the size of Massachusetts—since Japan in 1180 was about 15 times larger than that state. Given the difficulties of transportation and commu-nications, how could so few control such a large area? The answer is that they did not have to.

[1]H. Kitagawa and B. Tsuchida, trans., *The Tale of Heike* (Tokyo: Tokyo University Press, 1975), p. 330.

The local social order of the late Heian era continued into the Kamakura period. The Kyoto court, governors, district magistrates, and local notables—including many warriors who were not members of Yoritomo's band—functioned more or less as they had earlier. To protect their revenues from the land, they supported law and order. The Kamakura vassals newly appointed as military stewards and military governors had to win the cooperation of these local power-holders in order to establish their influence in the local society. In short, even if the Kamakura vassals could be called feudal, they were only a thin skim on the surface of a society constructed according to older principles.

Kamakura Rule After Yoritomo

As soon as Yoritomo died in 1199, his widow and her Hōjō kinsmen moved to usurp the power of the Minamoto house. The widow, having taken holy orders after her husband's death, was known as the Nun Shogun. One of her sons was pushed aside. The other became shogun but was murdered in 1219 by his mother's Hōjō kinsmen. After that, the Hōjō ruled as regents for a puppet shogun, just as the Fujiwara had been regents for figurehead emperors. The Kyoto court, trying to exploit the indignation aroused by this usurpation, led an armed suprising against Kamakura in 1221, but it was quickly suppressed. New military stewards were then placed on the lands of those who had joined in the uprising.

Any society based on personal bonds faces the problem of how to transfer loyalty from one generation to another. That the Kamakura vassals fought for the Hōjō in 1221, despite the Hōjō usurpation of Minamoto rule, suggests that their loyalty had become institutional. They were loyal to the *bakufu*, which guaranteed their income from land. Their personal loyalty to the Minamoto had ended with the death of Yoritomo.

A second challenge to Kamakura occurred in 1266, when Kublai Khan, the Mongol conqueror, sent envoys demanding that Japan submit to his rule. He had subjugated Korea in 1258, and his army looked outward across the Tsushima Straits. The Kyoto court was terrified, but the Hōjō at Kamakura refused to submit. The first Mongol invasion fleet arrived with 30,000 troops in 1274 but withdrew after initial victories. The Mongols again sent envoys; this time, they were beheaded. A second invasion force arrived in 1281, two years after Kublai completed his conquest of southern China. Carrying 140,000 troops, it was an amphibious operation on a scale unprecedented in world history. With gunpowder bombs and phalanxes of archers protected by a forward wall of soldiers carrying overlapping shields, the Mongol forces were formidable.

The Japanese tactics of fierce individual combat were not appropriate to their foe. But they erected a stone wall along the curved shoreline of Hakata Bay in northwestern Kyushu and held off the Mongols for two months until a typhoon, the *kamikaze,* or "divine winds," sank a portion of the Mongols' fleet and forced the rest to withdraw. Preparations for a third expedition ended with Kublai's death in 1294.

The burden of repelling the Mongols fell on Kamakura's vassals in Kyushu. Non-Kamakura warriors of Kyushu were also mobilized to fight under the command of military governors. But unlike 1221, there were no spoils of victory with which to reward those who had fought. Dissatisfaction was rife. Even temples and shrines demanded rewards, claiming that their prayers had brought about the divine winds.

Women in Warrior Society

Yoritomo's widow, the Nun Shogun, was one in a long line of important women in Japan. Although historians no longer speak of an early matriarchal age, there is no denying that the central figure of Japanese mythology was the sun goddess, who ruled the Plain of High Heaven. In the late Yayoi age, the shaman ruler Pimiko was probably not so unusual a figure; she was followed by the empresses of the Yamato and Nara courts, and they in turn by the great women writers of the Heian period. Under the Kamakura *bakufu,* there was only one Nun Shogun, but the daughters of warrior families often trained in archery and other military arts. Women also occasionally inherited the position of military steward. As long as society was stable, women fared relatively well. But as fighting became more common in the 14th century, their position began to decline; as warfare became endemic in the 15th, their status plummeted. A good part of the drop had to do with new rules of inheritance. The needs of warring feudal states dictated that all property and the military duties attached to it be passed on as a single parcel from father to son.

The Ashikaga Era

At times, formal political institutions seem rocklike in their stability, and history unfolds within the framework that they provide. Then, almost as if a kaleidoscope had been shaken, the old institutions collapse and are swept away. In their place appear new institutions and new patterns of personal relations that, often enough, had begun to take shape within the confines of the old. It is not easy to explain the timing of such upheavals, but they are easy to recognize. One occurred in Japan between 1331 and 1336.

Various tensions had developed within late Kamakura society. The patrimony of a warrior was divided among his children. Over several generations, vassals became poorer, often falling into debt. High-ranking vassals of Kamakura were dissatisfied with the Hōjō monopoly of key *bakufu* posts. In the meantime, the ties of vassals to

Kamakura were weakening, while the ties to other warriors within their region were growing stronger. New regional bands were ready to emerge. The precipitating event was a revolt in 1331 by Godaigo, an emperor who thought emperors should actually rule. Kamakura sent Ashikaga Takauji (1305–1358), the head of a branch family of the Minamoto line, to put down the revolt. Instead, he joined it, giving a clear signal to other regional lords, who threw off Kamakura's control and destroyed the Hōjō-controlled *bakufu*.

What emerged from the dust and confusion of the 1331–1336 revolt was a regional multistate system centering on Kyoto. Each region was governed by a warrior band about the size of the band that had brought Yorimoto to power a century and a half earlier. Ashikaga Takauji governed the central region about Kyoto. The offices of his *bakufu* were simple and functional: a samurai office for police and military matters, an administrative office for financial matters, a documents office for land records, and a judicial board to settle disputes. The offices were staffed by Takauji's vassals, with the most trusted vassals holding the highest posts. They were lords (now called *daimyō*) in their own right and usually held concurrent appointments as military governors in the provinces surrounding Kyoto. The *bakufu* also appointed vassals to watch over its interests in the far north, in eastern Japan, and in Kyushu.

Government in outlying regions was diverse. Some lords held several provinces, others only one. Some had integrated most of the warriors in their areas into their own bands. Others had unassimilated military bands within their territories, forcing them to rely more on the authority of Kyoto. Formally, all regional lords or daimyo were the vassals of the shogun, but the relationship was often nominal. Some regional lords lived on their lands, some lived in Kyoto.

The relationship between the Kyoto *bakufu* and the regional lords fluctuated during the 1336–1467 period. At times, able lords made their regions into virtually independent states. At other times, the Kyoto *bakufu* became stronger. The third shogun, Ashikaga Yoshimitsu, for example, tightened his grip on the Kyoto court. He even relinquished the military post of shogun, giving it to his son in 1394, in order to take the highest civil post of grand minister of state. He also improved relations with the great Buddhist temples and Shinto shrines and established ties with the Ming China. Most significant were his military campaigns, which dented the autonomy of regional lords outside the inner Kyoto circle.

But even the third shogun had to rely on his daimyo vassals. To strengthen them for his military campaigns, he permitted them to levy taxes and control all judical and administrative offices in their regions, and to take on unaffiliated warriors as direct vassals. Over generations, as ties of personal loyalty between daimyo and shogun weakened, these powers made the daimyo virtually independent. One level down, the ties of loyalty between samurai retainers and their daimyo were also growing weaker, and new bands of local warriors began to form in the interstices of the daimyo regional states.

Military House Rule: Taira, Minamoto, and Ashikaga (1160–1467)

1160–1180	Taira rule in Kyoto
1185–1333	Kamakura *bakufu*
1185	Founded by Minamoto Yoritomo
1219	Usurped by Hōjō
1221	Uprising by court
1232	Formation of Jōei Code
1274 and 1281	Invasion by Mongols
1336–1467	Ashikaga *bakufu*
1336	Begun by Ashikaga Takauji
1392	End of Southern Court
1467	Start of Warring States era

Agriculture, Commerce, and Medieval Guilds

Population figures for medieval Japan are rough estimates at best, but recent scholarship suggests 6 million for the year 1200 and 12 million for 1600. Much of the increase occurred during the late Kamakura and Ashikaga periods, when the country was fairly peaceful. The increase was brought about by land reclamation and improvements in agricultural technology. Iron-edged tools became available to all. New strains of rice were developed. Irrigation and diking improved. Double cropping began with vegetables planted during the fall and winter in dry fields, which were then flooded and planted with rice during the spring and summer.

In the Nara and early Heian periods, the economy was almost exclusively agricultural. Japan had no money, little commerce, and no cities of importance—apart from Nara, which developed into a temple town living on assigned revenues, and Kyoto, where taxes were consumed. Following the example of China, the government had established a mint, but little money actually circulated. Taxes were paid in grain and labor. Commercial transactions were largely barter, with silk or grain as the medium of exchange. Artisans produced for the noble households or temples to which they were attached. Peasants were economically self-sufficient.

From the late Heian period, partly as a side effect of fixed tax quotas, more of the growing agricultural surplus stayed in local hands. This trend accelerated during the Kamakura and Ashikaga periods, when land income shifted from court aristocrats to warriors. As this transfer occurred, artisans detached themselves from noble households and began to produce for the market. Military equipment was an early staple of commerce, but gradually *sake*, lumber, paper, vegetable oils, salt, and products of the sea also became commercialized. A demand for copper coins appeared, and since they were no longer minted in Japan, they were imported in increasingly huge quantities from China.

During the Kamakura period, independent merchants emerged to handle the products of artisans. Some trade networks spread over all of Japan. More often, artisan and merchant guilds, not unlike those of medieval Europe, paid a fee in exchange for monopoly rights in a given area. Early Kyoto guilds paid fees to powerful nobles or temples, and later to the Ashikaga *bakufu*. In outlying areas, guild privileges were obtained from the regional feudal lords. From the Kamakura period onward, markets were held periodically in many parts of Japan, often by a river or at a crossroads. Some place names in Japan today reveal such an origin. Yokkaichi, today an industrial city, means "fourth-day market." It began as a market held on the 4th, 14th, and 24th days of each month. During the 14th and 15th centuries such markets were held with increasing frequency until, eventually, permanent towns were established.

BUDDHISM AND MEDIEVAL CULTURE

The Nara and Heian periods are usually referred to as Japan's classical age. The period that followed—from about 1200 to 1600—is often called medieval. It was medieval in the root sense of the word in that it lay between the other two major spans of premodern Japanese history. It was also medieval in that it shared some characteristics that we label medieval in Europe and China. However, there is an important difference. Medieval Japan was a direct outgrowth of classical Japan; one can even say that there was an overlap during the early Kamakura. In contrast, Europe was torn by barbarian invasions, and a millennium separated the classical culture of Rome from high medieval culture. Even to have a Charlemagne, Europe had to wait for half a millennium. In China, too, the era of political disunity and barbarian invasions lasted 400 years, and it was during these years that its medieval Buddhist culture blossomed.

The results of the historical continuity in Japan are visible in every branch of its culture. The earlier poetic tradition continued with great vigor. In 1205 the compilation of the *New Collection from Ancient and Modern Times (Shinkokinshū)* was ordered by the same emperor who began the 1221 rebellion against Kamakura. The flat *Yamato-e* style of painting that had reached a peak in the early 12th-century *Genji Scrolls* continued into the medieval era with scrolls on historical and religious themes or fairy-tale adventures. Artisanal skills continued without a break. The same techniques of lacquerwork with inlaid mother-of-pearl that had been employed, say, to make a cosmetic box for a Heian court lady were now used to produce saddles for Kamakura warriors. In short, just as Heian estates and the authority of the Kyoto court continued into the Kamakura era, so also did Heian culture extend into medieval Japan.

Nonetheless, medieval Japanese culture had some distinctly new characteristics. First, as the leadership of the society shifted from court aristocrats to military aristocrats, new forms of literature appeared. The medieval military tales were as different from the *Tale of Genji* as the armor of the mounted warrior was from the no-less-colorful silken robes of the court nobility. Second, a new wave of culture entered from China. If the Nara and Heian had been shaped by T'ang culture, medieval Japan—although not its institutions—was shaped by Sung culture. This link is immediately apparent in the ink paintings of medieval era. Third, and most important, the medieval centuries were Japan's age of Buddhist faith. A religious revolution occurred during the Kamakura period and deepened during the Ashikaga. It powerfully influenced the arts of Japan.

Japanese Pietism: Pure Land and Nichiren Buddhism

Among the doctrines of the Heian Tendai sect was the belief that the true teachings of the historical Buddha had been lost and that salvation could be had only by calling on the name of Amida, the Buddha who ruled over the Western Paradise (or Pure Land). During the 10th and 11th centuries, itinerant preachers began to spread Pure Land doctrines and practices beyond the narrow circles of Kyoto. Kūya (903–972), the "saint of the marketplace," for example, preached not only in Kyoto and throughout the provinces, but even to the aboriginal Ainu in northernmost Japan. The doctrine that the world had fallen on evil times and that only faith would suffice was given credence by earthquakes, epidemics, fires, and banditry in the capital, as well as wars throughout the land. The deepening Buddhist coloration of the age can be read in the opening lines of the 13th-century *Tale of Heike*, a military chronicle written just two centuries after the *Tale of Genji* and the *Pillow Book*:

> The sound of the bell of Jetavana echoes the impermanence of all things. The hue of the flowers of the teak-tree declares that they who flourish must be brought low. Yea, the proud ones are but for a moment, like an evening dream in springtime. The mighty are destroyed at the last, they are but as the dust before the wind.[2]

In the early Kamakura era, two figures stand out as religious geniuses who experienced the truth of Pure Land Buddhism within themselves. Hōnen (1133–1212) was perhaps the first to say that the invocation of the name of Amida alone was enough for salvation and that only faith, and not good works or rituals, counted. These claims brought Hōnen into conflict with the older Buddhist establishment and marked the emergence of Pure Land as a separate sect. Hōnen was followed by Shinran

[2]A. L. Sadler, trans., *The Tenfoot Square Hut and Tales of the Heike* (Rutland, VT, and Tokyo: Charles E. Tuttle, 1972), p. 22.

(1173–1262), who taught that even a single invocation in praise of Amida, if done with perfect faith, was sufficient for salvation. But perfect faith was not the result of human effort; it was a gift from Amida. Shinran taught that pride was an obstacle to purity of heart. One of his famous sayings is, "If even a good man can be reborn in the Pure Land, how much more so a wicked man."[3] Shinran is saying that the evil man is less inclined to assume that he is the source of his own salvation and therefore more inclined to place his complete trust in Amida.

Shinran's emphasis on faith alone led him to break many of the monastic rules of earlier Buddhism: he ate meat; he married a nun, and thereafter the Pure Land sect had a married clergy; he taught that all occupations were equally "heavenly" if performed with a pure heart. Exiled from Kyoto, he traveled about Japan establishing "True Pure Land" congregations. (When the Jesuits arrived in Japan in the 16th century, they called this sect "the devil's Christianity.")

As a result of a line of distinguished teachers after Shinran, its doctrinal simplicity, and its reliance on the practice of piety, Pure Land Buddhism became the dominant form of Buddhism in Japan and remains so today. It was also the only sect in medieval Japan—apart from the Tendai sect on Mount Hiei—to develop political and military power. As a religion of faith, it developed a strong church as a protection for the saved while they were still in this world. As peasants became partially militarized during the 15th century, some Pure Land village congregations created self-defense forces. At times, they rebelled against feudal lords. In one instance, Pure Land armies ruled the province of Kaga for over a century. These congregations were smashed during the late 16th century wars of unification, and the sect depoliticized.

A second devotional sect was founded by Nichiren (1222–1282), who believed that the Lotus Sutra perfectly embodied the teachings of Buddha. He instructed his adherents to chant, over and over, "Praise to the Lotus Sutra of the Wondrous Law," usually to the accompaniment of rapid drumbeats. Like the repetition of "Praise to the Amida Buddha" in the Pure Land sect or comparable verbal formulas in other religions around the world, the chanting optimally induced a state of religious rapture. The goal of an internal spiritual transformation was common to both the devotional and the meditative sects of Buddhism. Nichiren was remarkable for a Buddhist in being intolerant and nationalistic. He blamed the ills of his age on rival sects and asserted that only his sect could protect Japan. He predicted the Mongol invasions, and his sect claimed credit for the "divine winds" that sank the Mongol fleets. Even his adopted Buddhist name, Nichiren or "Sun Lotus," combined the character for the rising sun of Japan with that of the flower symbolizing Buddhism.

[3]R. Tsunoda, W. T. de Bary, and D. Keene, eds., *Sources of the Japanese Tradition* (New York: Columbia University Press, 1958), p. 217.

Zen Buddhism

Meditation had long been a part of Japanese monastic practice. Zen meditation and doctrines were introduced by monks returning from study in Sung China. Eisai (1141–1215) transposed to Japan the Rinzai sect in 1191 and Dōgen (1200–1253) the Sōtō sect in 1227. Eisai's sect was patronized by the Hōjō rulers in Kamakura and the

A winter landscape by the Zen monk Sesshū (1420–1506). Ink on paper. [Tokyo National Museum]

The Arts and Zen Buddhism

Zen Buddhism in Japan developed a theory of art that influenced every department of high medieval culture. Put simply , the theory is that intuitive action is better than conscious, purposive action. The best painter is one so skilled that he no longer needs to think of technique but paints as a natural act. Substitute a sword for a brush, and the same theory applies: a warrior who has to stop to consider his next move is at a disadvantage in battle. To this emphasis on direct, intuitive action is added the Zen distinction between the deluded mind and the "original mind." The latter is also referred to as the "no mind," or the mind in the enlightened state. The highest intuitive action proceeds from such a state of being. This theory was applied, in time, to the performance of the actor, to the skill of the potter, to archery, to flower arrangement, and to the tea ceremony. Compare the following two passages, one by Seami (1363–1443), the author of many Nō plays, and the other by Takuan Sōhō (1573–1645), a famous Zen master of the early Tokugawa era.

Could the same theory be applied to baseball? If it were, would baseball change?

1. Sometimes spectators of the Nō say, "The moments of 'no-action' are the most enjoyable." This is an art which the actor keeps secret. Dancing and singing, movements and the different types of miming are all acts performed by the body. Moments of "no-action" occur in between. When we examine why such movements without actions are enjoyable, we find that it is due to the underlying spiritual strength of the actor which

Ashikaga in Kyoto. Dōgen established his sect on Japan's western coast, far from centers of political power.

Zen was a religion of paradox. Its monks were learned, yet it stressed a return to ignorance, to the uncluttered "original mind," attained in a flash of intuitive understanding. Zen was punctiliously traditional, the most Chinese of Japanese medieval sects. The authority of the Zen master over his pupil-monks was absolute. Yet Zen was also iconoclastic. Its sages were depicted in paintings as tearing up sutras to make the point that it is religious experience and not words that count. Within the rigidly structured monastic regimen, a give-and-take occurred as Zen masters tested the pupil-monks understanding of Buddhism, gained through long hours of meditation, in individual encounters. Buddhism stressed compassion for all sentient beings, yet in Japan the Zen sect included many samurai whose duty was to fight and kill. A few military leaders encouraged the practice of Zen among their retainers in the hope of instilling a single-minded attention to duty; a handful of Hōjō and Ashikaga rulers even went so far as to practice Zen meditation.

unremittingly holds the attention. He does not relax the tension when the dancing or singing come to an end or at intervals between the dialogue and the different types of miming, but maintains an unwavering inner strength. This feeling of inner strength will faintly reveal itself and bring enjoyment. However, it is undesirable for the actor to permit this inner strength to become obvious to the audience. If it is obvious, it becomes an act, and is no longer "no-actin." The actions before and after an interval of "no-action" must be linked by entering the state of mindlessness in which one conceals even from oneself one's intent. This, then, is the faculty of moving audiences, by linking all the artistic powers with one mind.

2. Where should a swordsman fix his mind? If he puts his mind on the physical movement of his opponent, it will be seized by the movement; if he places it on the sword of his opponent, it will be arrested by the sword; if he focuses his mind on the thought of striking his opponent, it will be carried away by the very thought; if the mind stays on his own sword, it will be captured by his sword; if he centers it on the thought of not being killed by his opponent, his mind will be overtaken by this very thought; if he keeps his mind firmly on his own or on his opponent's posture, likewise, it will be blocked by them. Thus the mind should not be fixed anywhere.

1. From *Sources of Japanese Tradition*, trans. by William Theodore de Bary. Copyright 1958 by Columbia University. Reprinted with permission of the publisher .

2. From *The Buddhist Tradition* by William Theodore de Bary. Copyright 1969 by Wiliam Theodore de Bary. Reprinted by permission of Random House Inc.

A notable aspect of Zen was its influence on the arts of medieval Japan. It did not create them, but it shaped them to its tastes. The most beautiful gardens, for example, were in Zen temples. Many were designed by Zen masters. The most famous, at Ryōanji, consists of 15 rocks set in white sand. Others only slightly less austere contain moss, shrubs, trees, ponds, and streams. With these elements and within a small compass, rocks become cliffs, raked sand becomes rivers or the sea, and a little world of nature emerges. If a garden may be said to possess philosophic stillness, the Zen gardens of Daitokuji and other Kyoto temples have it.

Zen monks such as Josetsu, Shūbun (ca. 1415), and Sesshū (1420–1506) certainly number among the masters of ink painting in East Asia. One painting by Josetsu shows a man trying to catch a catfish with a gourd. Like the sound of one hand clapping, the impossibility of catching a catfish with a gourd presents as art the kind of logical conundrum used to expound Zen teachings. Sesshū painted in both the broken-ink style, in which splashlike brush strokes represent an entire mountain landscape, and a more usual calligraphic style. Because the artist's creativity was seen as grounded in his experience

Detail of a Portrait of Ikkyū Sōjun
(1394–1481) by Bakusai. In the *Kyoto
National Museum Collection.*

of meditation, a painting of a waterfall or a crow on a leafless branch in late autumn was
viewed as no less religious than a painting of the mythic Zen founder Bodhidharma.

Nō Plays

Another fascinating product of Ashikaga culture was the Nō play, a kind of mystery
drama without parallels elsewhere in East Asia. The play was performed on a square, bare
wooden stage (usually outdoors) by male actors wearing robes of great beauty and carved,
painted masks of enigmatic expressions. Many such masks and robes number among
Japan's "national treasures." The chorus was chanted to the accompaniment of flute and
drums. The language was poetic. The action was slow and highly stylized: circling about
the stage could represent a journey; a motion of the hand, the reading of a letter. At a critical juncture in most plays, the protagonist was possessed by the spirit of another and performed a dance. Spirit possession was commonplace in Japanese folk religion and also
occurred in the *Tale of Genji*. Several plays were shown in a single performance; comic skits
called "Crazy Words" were usually interspersed between the plays to break the tension.

Nō plays reveal a medley of themes present in medieval Japanese culture. Some
pivot on incidents in the struggle between the Taira and the Minamoto. Some are religious: a cormorant fisher is saved from the king of hell for having given lodging to a

Hakuin's Enlightenenment

Hakuin (1686–1769) was a poet, a painter, and a Zen master. He wrote in colloquial Japanese as well as in Chinese. He illustrated the continuing power of the Zen tradition in postmedieval times. The following passages are from an autobiographical account of his spiritual quest. The first follows a recounting of his disappointments and failures and tells of his initial enlightenment. His teacher did not accept this as adequate, however: The second passage tells of his experience eight years later.

1.

In the spring of my twenty-fourth year, I was painfully struggling at the Eiganji in the province of Echigo. I slept neither day nor night, forgetting either to eat or sleep. A great doubt suddenly possessed me, and I felt as if frozen to death in the midst of an icy field extending thousands of *li*. A sense of an extraordinary purity permeated my bosom. I could not move. I was virtually senseless. What remained was only *Mu*. Although I heard the master's lectures in the Lecture Hall, it was as though I were listening to his disclosure from some sixty or seventy steps outside the Hall, or as if I were floating in the air. This condition lasted for several days until one night I heard the striking of a temple bell. All at once a transformation came over me, as though a layer of ice were smashed or a tower of jade pulled down. Instantly I came to my senses. Former doubts were completely dissolved, like ice which had melted away. "How marvelous! How marvelous!" I cried out aloud. There was no cycle of birth and death from which I had to escape, no enlightenment for which I had to seek.

2.

At the age of thirty-two I settled in this dilapidated temple [Shoinji]. In a dream one night my mother handed me a purple silk robe. When I lifted it I felt great weights in both sleeves. Examining it, I found in each sleeve an old mirror about five or six inches in diameter. The reflection of the right-hand mirror penetrated deep into my heart. My own mind, as well as mountains and rivers, the entire earth, became serene and bottomless. The left-hand mirror had no luster on its entire surface. Its face was like that of a new iron pan not yet touched by fire. Suddenly I became aware that the luster on the left-hand mirror surpassed that of the right by a million times. After this incident, the vision of all things was like looking at my own face. For the first time I realized the meaning of the words, "The eyes of the Tatha-gata behold the Buddha-nature."

priest. Some plays pick up incidents from the *Tale of Genji* or the Heian court: the famous Heian beauty and poet Ono no Komachi is possessed by the spirit of a lover she had spurned; their conflict is left to be resolved in a Buddhist afterlife. The Buddhist idea of impermanence, of this world as a place of suffering, and of the need to relinquish worldly attachments is found in many plays. Some plays are close to fairy tales: a fisherman takes the feather robe of an angel, but when she begins to sicken and grow wan, he returns the robe and she performs for him a dance that is performed only in heaven. Some plays are based on stories from China: a traveler dreams an entire lifetime on a magical pillow while waiting for a bowl of millet to cook. Another play reflects the constant Japanese ambivalence toward Chinese culture from which Japan had borrowed so much: Po Chu-i, the T'ang poet most esteemed in Japan, rows a boat over the seas and comes to the shores of Japan, where he is met by fishermen who turn him back in the name of Japanese poetry. One fisherman speaks:

> You in China make your poems and odes out of the Scriptures of India; and we have made our "*uta*" out of the poems and odes of China. Since then our poetry is a blend of three lands, we have named it Yamato, the great blend, and all our songs "Yamato uta."[4]

At the end, a fisherman is transformed into the Shinto god of Japanese poetry and performs the "Sea Green Dance."

WARRING STATES ERA (1467–1600)

War is the universal solvent of old institutions. Nowhere in history is this clearer than in Japan between 1467 and 1568. In 1467 a succession dispute arose over who would be the next Ashikaga shogun. The dispute led to war between two territorial lords who supported the respective contenders. Other lords used the opportunity to gain territory at the expense of weaker neighbors, and wars raged throughout Japan for 11 years. Most of Kyoto was destroyed in the fighting, and the authority of the Ashikaga *bakufu* came to an end. This first war ended in 1477, but after a pause the fighting resumed and continued for more than a century.

War of All Against All

Even before 1467 the Ashikaga equilibrium had been precarious. Regional daimyo lords had relied on their relationship to the *bakufu* to hold their stronger

[4]A. Waley, trans., *The Nō Plays of Japan* (New York: Grove Press, 1957), p. 252.

vassals in check, while relying on those vassals to preserve their independence against strong neighbors. The collapse of *bakufu* authority after 1467 pulled the linchpin from the system. It left the regional lords standing alone, removing the last barrier to wars among them.

Regional lords, however, were too weak to stand alone. A region was a hodge-podge of competing jurisdictions. Lands might be "public" and still pay some taxes to Kyoto, or they might be estates, and some were beginning to look like private fiefs. Revenues might be paid to nobles in Kyoto, to regional lords, or to local samurai strongmen. Most regions contained military bands that were not the vassals of the daimyo. Several daimyo had lands in territories of other lords. Occasionally vassals were militarily more powerful than their *daimyo* lords. Some local vassals commanded bands of village warriors. Once the regional *daimyo* were forced to stand alone, they became prey to the stronger among their vassals as well as to neighboring states.

By the end of the 16th century all Ashikaga *daimyo* had fallen, with one exception in remote southern Kyushu. In their place emerged hundreds of little "warring states *daimyo*," each with his own warrior band. In one prefecture on the Inland Sea, the remains of 200 hillside castles of such *daimyo* have been identified. The constant wars among these men were not unlike those of the early feudal era in Europe.

A Japanese expression for "the survival of the fittest"—"the strong eat and the weak become the meat"—is often applied to this century of warfare. Of the *daimyo* bands, the most efficient in revamping their domain for military ends survived. The less ruthless, who clung to old ways, were defeated and absorbed. It was an age, as one Warring States general put it, "when only muscle counts." Another said, "The warrior doesn't care if he's called a dog or beast, the main thing is winning."[5]

Early in this period, when there were hundreds of contending small states and surprise attacks were frequent, castles were built on a bluff above a river or on a mountainside with natural defenses. Inuyama Castle, today a 30-minute bus ride from Nagoya, is the most impressive surviving example. While rougher and less elaborate than the castles of a century later, it is a real fort built to withstand an enemy attack.

As fighting continued, hundreds of local states gave way to tens of regional states. The castles of such regional states were often located on plains. As castletowns grew up around them, merchants flocked to supply the needs of their growing soldiery. Alliances of these regional states fought it out, until in the late 16th century, all of Japan was brought under the hegemony of a single overlord. Oda Nobunaga (1534–1582) unified most of central Japan; Toyotomi Hideyoshi (1535–1598), the entire country; and, after Hideyoshi's death and the breakup of his alliance, Tokugawa Ieyasu (1542–1616) reestablished a unified Japan.

[5]G. Elison and B. L. Smith (eds.) *Warlords, Artists and Commoners* (Honolulu, Hawaii University Press, 1981) p. 57.

Lord Sōun's Precepts

Warring States daimyo often wrote "house laws" or codes of behavior for the edification of their retainers. Hōjō Sōun (1432?–1519) rose late in life to become a *daimyo*-lord. He reduced the taxes on peasants in his dormain and shared the spoils of war with his retainers. Several of the 21 articles in his code are cited below.

How do there moral injunctions prepare samurai *to serve their lord?*

Item: Above all, have faith in the Buddha and in Shinto deities.

Item: Rise, yes, very early in the morning. If you rise late, even your servants will become lax and unusable. You will be failing to do your duties, both official and private. If this begins to happen, you are bound to be given up by your master, so be extremely careful.

Item: Offering prayers is for your own sake. Simply keep your mind straight and pliant, honest and law-abiding. Be respectful to those who are above you, and be compassionate to those who are below you. Accept things as they are: what you have as what you have, what you don't as what you don't. Doing so seems to accord with the wishes of the Buddha and Shinto deities. Even if you don't pray, by keeping this in mind you will enjoy various deities' protection.

Item: Don't think your swords and clothes should be as good as those of other people. Be content as long as they don't look awful. Once you start acquiring what you don't have and become even poorer, you'll become a laughingstock.

Item: Whenever you have a little bit of time for yourself, read a book. Always carry something with characters written on it with you and look at it when no one's looking. Unless you accustom yourself to

Foot-Soldier Revolution

During the Warring States period, the foot soldier replaced the mounted warrior as the backbone of the military in Japan. Soldiers were still called samurai. They were still the vassals of *daimyo* or, sometimes, the vassals of vassals of *daimyo*. But their numbers, social status, and techniques of warfare changed dramatically. As a result, Japanese society changed from what it had been only a century earlier.

The changes began on the land. Ashikaga *daimyo* had diverted more and more land revenues for their own use, but Warring States *daimyo* took them all. Public lands and estates, including those of the imperial house, were seized and converted into fiefs. Soldiers were paid stipends from the revenues of the *daimyo's* lands, and important vassals, usually the officers or commanders of the *daimyo's*

them, asleep or awake, you'll forget them. The same is true of writing.

Item: Never say a single word of falsehood or even half of it to anyone, high or low. Even when joking, tell the truth. If you continue to say false things, it will become your habit and people will begin to torment you. In the end they'll give up on you. You must be prepared to think it a disgrace for your lifetime if someone accuses you.

Item: Whenever you have time off from your service to your master, work at horse-riding. Learn the basics from an expert, and learn the handling of the reins and other things on your own.

Item: Seek good friends in writing and learning. Avoid bad friends in go, chess, pipes, and flutes. Not knowing these things is not a disgrace for you, nor is there evil in learning them. It's simply that you'd rather not waste your time on them.

Whenever three people take a road, there's always one who's worthy as a teacher. Choose that one person and follow him. By looking at the one who isn't good, you correct your ways.

Item: In the evening, check yourself the sources of fire in the kitchen and your wife's room, firmly tell her to be careful, and make a habit of taking preventive measures against a fire from your neighbors. Do this every night. Noble or lowly, wives tend to have no thought about these things and to be lax, leaving valuables and clothes scattered about.

Even if you have servants, don't think only of telling them to do everything. Do things yourself first so that you may know what they're like. Only then think of having others do them.

Item: Always work at reading, writing, martial skills, archery, and horse-riding. There is no need to detail this. Hold literary skills in your left hand, martial skills in your right. This is the law from ancient times. Never neglect it.

Hiroaki Sato, *Legends of the Samurai* (Copyright © 1995), pp. 249–253. Reprinted with permission of The Overlook Press.

army, were awarded fiefs of their own. The governance of fiefs was essentially private, in the hands of the fief holder. Inheritance patterns changed to fit the new circumstances. Multigeniture—the division of a warrior's rights to revenues from land among his children—was not appropriate to a society with a hereditary military class. To protect the integrity of the warrior's household economy, multigeniture had begun to give way to single inheritance during the Ashikaga period. After 1467 single inheritance became universal. As the fief was often passed to the most able son, not necessarily the eldest, the pattern is usually called *unigeniture* rather than *primogeniture*.

With larger revenues, Warring States *daimyo* built bigger armies. They recruited mainly from the peasantry. Some of the new soldiers moved to the castle town of the *daimyo*. Others lived on the land or remained in their villages, farming in peace and fighting in war. The growth of the military class had begun earlier. Accounts of 12th-

Takeda Shingen

The Warring States era was an age of treachery, cruelty, and changing loyalties, when every enemy was a potential ally and every ally a potential enemy. Takeda Shingen (1521–1573), the *daimyo*-lord of Kai, a province in eastern Japan, was famous both as a general and as a wise ruler. The "Iron Battle Fan" describes a scene in the battle against Shingen's enemy. Uesugi Kenshin, another famous warrior-general.

What do the following passages tell you of the concerns of the lords of 16th-century Japan?

How to Rule a Country: A Verse

The people are the castle, the stone wall,
    and the moat;
compassion makes a friend, vengeance a
    foe

On Making War

Shingen constantly read a range of books. He took Sun Tzu's words and had them written on his flag: "Immovable as a mountain, destructive as fire, quiet as a forest, swift as a wind." Baba Nobufusa once asked, "Sir, the wind may be swift, but doesn't it cease as soon as it rises?" Shingen said, "In moving an army I'd like to be as swift as I can. Should I have to cease, my second in command would continue." Nobufusa said, "You would then be counting on the second round for victory." In that way the master and his subjects investigated military matters. Everything was done in that fashion.

The Iron Battle Fan

. . . Almost at once, one unit of Kenshin's aides-de-camp turned around to the right of Shingen's camp, drove off Lord Yoshinobu's fifty mounted aides-de-camp, along with about 400 troops, and cut into Lord Shingen's aides-de-camp. 3,600 or 3,700 soldiers, friends and foes combined, were thrown into a melee, stabbing and getting stabbed, slashing and getting slashed, some grabbing each other's armored shoulders,

century battles tell of fighting by tens or hundreds of warriors, sometimes more. Scroll paintings of the Heiji wars corroborate these figures. By the 14th century, battles involved thousands or tens of thousands of troops. By the late 16th century, hundreds of thousands were deployed in major campaigns. Screen paintings show massed troops in fixed emplacements with officers riding about on horseback. Of course, special cavalry strike forces were still used.

In the mid-14th century, a new weapon was developed: a thrusting spear with a thick shaft and a heavy chisel-like blade. Held in both hands, it could penetrate medieval armor as a sword could not. It could also be swung about like a quarterstaff. It was used by soldiers positioned at intervals of three feet, in a pin-cushion tactic to impale charging cavalry. The weapon spelled the end of the aristocratic warrior in Japan, just as the pikes used by Swiss soldiers ended knighthood in northern Europe during the 15th century.

grappling and falling down; one would take his enemy's head and rise to his feet, when someone, shouting, "That's my master's head," would skewer him with his spear, and a third, seeing that, would cut that man down. The Kai forces were so taken up by what was happening right in front of them they didn't even know where Lord Shingen was. The same was true of the Echigo forces.

At that moment a warrior wearing a pale-green sleeveless jacket, his head wrapped in a white kerchief, riding a light cream-colored horse, a three-foot drawn sword in hand, galloped straight up to Lord Shingen, who was sitting in his chair, struck at him three times, barely missing him each time. Lord Shingen stopped the blows with his battle-fan. When later examined, the fan had eight sword cuts. His chief attendant and the head of his twenty-man bodyguard, twenty men in all, each a brave warrior, ferociously fought back, even while surrounding him lest friends or foes spot him, cutting down anyone who came close. Ōsumi Governor Hara, the chief attendant, took up Lord Shingen's spear, which had

blue shells inlaid in its handle, and stabbed at the warrior in the pale-green sleeveless damask jacket on the light cream-colored horse. He missed. He stabbed at the top of the warrior's armor but hit the forward part of his horse's rump. The horse reared straight up, then bolted. When later inquired about, the warrior turned out to be no other than Terutora [Kenshin].

Among Lord Shingen's aides-de-camp, Obu Saburō, of the Middle Palace Guards, along with his men, repelled Echigo's first spearhead, Kakizaki and his men, and pursued them for about 300 yards. Anayama and his men, too, pursued Kenshin's retainer, Shibata, for about 400 yards. All that while Lord Shingen had only his chief attendant, twenty-man bodyguard, and seventeen or eighteen pages, Tsuchiya Heihachi and Naoda Kihei among them, but would not withdraw a single step, standing at the spot where he rose from his chair.

Hiroaki Sato, *Legends of the Samurai* (Copyright © 1995), pp. 204, 224–225, 21–219. Reprinted with permission of The Overlook Press.

After 1467 this spear became the principal weapon of Warring States Japan. Not surprisingly, its spread coincided with the recruitment of peasant soldiers, for it required only short training. By the early 16th century, it was every warrior's dream to be the "number one spearsman" of his lord. Even generals trained in its use. One famous general wrote that "one hundred spearsmen are more effective than ten thousand swords."

A second change was the introduction of the musket by the Portuguese in the mid-16th century. It was quickly adopted by Warring States generals. Its superiority was proved in the Battle of Nagashino in 1575, in which Oda Nobunaga and Tokugawa Ieyasu used spear and musket platoons against the cavalry of a famous military tactician. Massing 3000 muskets behind a bamboo barrier-fence and firing in volleys, Nobunaga decimated the forces of his enemy. As individual combat gave way to mass armies, warfare became pitiless, cruel, and bloody.

Piracy, Trade, and Foreign Relations

Commerce continued to grow during the Warring States era. It is unclear why it was not stunted by the frequent wars. One possible reason is that great battles only rarely ravaged the free ports and castletowns where merchants were based. Another was the stimulus of foreign trade. The content of the trade reflected the progress of Japanese crafts. Early Japanese exports to China had been raw materials such as copper, sulphur, or silver, but by the 16th century manufactured goods were rising in importance and included swords, spears, wine bottles, folding fans, picture scrolls, screen paintings, ink slabs, and the like. In exchange, Japan received copper cash, porcelains, paintings, books, and medicines.

During the centuries before unification, Japanese pirate-traders plied the seas of East Asia, often raiding Chinese coastal cities. To halt their depredations, the Ming emperor had invited the third shogun, Ashikaga Yoshimitsu, to trade with China. An agreement was reached in 1404, and the Ming emperor appointed Yoshimitsu the "King of Japan." During the next century and a half, periodic "tribute missions" were sent to China. The opening of official trade channels did not, however, end piracy. It stopped only after Japan was reunified at the close of the 16th century.

The first unifier, Hideyoshi, permitted only ships with his vermilion seal to trade with China. The Tokugawa, who followed Hideyoshi, continued his policy after 1600. Between 1604 and 1635 over 350 ships went to China in this "vermilion-seal trade." Then, in 1635 the imposition of seclusion brought Japan's foreign trade to a gradual halt: Japanese were prohibited from leaving Japan; the construction of large ships was prohibited; trade with the continent was limited to a small community of Chinese merchants in Nagasaki and to clandestine trading with China through the Ryukyu Islands and with Korea through the Tsushima Islands.

Overlapping Japan's maritime expansion in the seas of East Asia was the arrival of European ships. Portuguese pirate-traders made their way to Goa in India, to Malacca, to Macao in China, and arrived in Japan in 1543. Spanish galleons came in 1587 via Mexico and the Philippines. These eastern and western waves of Iberian expansion were followed by the Dutch and the English after the turn of the century.

The Portuguese, from a tiny country with a population of 1.5 million, were motivated by a desire for booty and profits and by religious zeal. Their ships were superior. Taking advantage of the Chinese ban on maritime commerce, they became important as shippers. They carried Southeast Asian goods and Japanese silver to China and Chinese silk to Japan, and they used their profits to buy Southeast Asian spices for the European market. The Portuguese, initially at least, found it easier to trade with the daimyo of a disunited Japan than to deal with the authorities of a united China. A few Kyushu daimyo, thinking to attract Portuguese traders, even converted to Christianity.

"The Arrival of the Portuguese in Japan." Portuguese merchants arrived in Japan in 1543 from India and the East Indies.   Their crews were multi-ethnic, and they brought Jesuit priests as well. [Giraudon/Art Resource, N.Y.]

Traders brought with them Jesuit missionaries. The Society of Jesus had been founded in 1540 to act as "soldiers" in the pope's campaign against the Reformation. Only nine years later, Saint Francis Xavier (1506–1552) arrived in Japan. He soon wrote back that the Japanese were "the best [people] who have yet been discovered." Another Jesuit wrote that the Japanese "are all white, courteous, and highly civilized, so much so that they surpass all other known races of the world." The Japanese, for their part, appeared to admire the Jesuits for their asceticism, devoutness, and learning.

As they had attempted to convert scholar-officials in China, so the Jesuits in Japan directed their efforts toward the samurai. Moving to Kyoto, they won the favor of Nobunaga, who was engaged in campaigns against warrior monks on Mount Hiei and against Pure Land strongholds in Osaka. Portuguese and Christian objects became fashionable. Painters produced "Southern Barbarian screens" that depicted the "black ships" of the Portuguese. Christian symbols were used on lacquer boxes and saddles. Nobunaga himself occasionally wore Portuguese clothes and a cross and said he might become a Christian if only the Jesuits would drop their insistence on monogamy. Christian converts increased from a few in the early years to 130,000 in 1579 and about 300,000 in 1600. That is to say, in the late 16th century a higher percentage of Japanese were Christian than today.

It is difficult to explain why Christianity met with greater success in Japan than in other East Asian lands. When introduced, it was seen as a new Buddhist sect. There seemed little difference to the Japanese between the cosmic Buddha of Shingon and the Christian God, between the paradise of Amida and the Christian heaven, or between prayers to Kannon—the female *bodhisattva* of mercy—and to the Virgin Mary. The Japanese also noted the theological similarity between the pietism of the Pure Land sect and that of Christianity. To Japanese ears, the passage in Romans 10:13, "whosoever shall call upon the name of the Lord shall be saved," was reminiscent of the Pure Land practice of invoking the name of Amida. The Jesuits, too, noted these parallels and felt that the devil had established these sects in Japan to test their faith. Xavier, who, despite his admirable personal characteristics, was narrow-minded, referred to the historical Buddha and Amida as "two demons." Although this intolerance gave rise to tensions and animosities, Christianity spread, to no small measure as a result of the personal example of the Jesuits. The fortunes of Christianity began to decline in 1597, when Hideyoshi banned Christianity and had 6 Spanish Franciscans and 20 Japanese converts crucified in Nagasaki. Hideyoshi was aware of Spanish colonialism in the Philippines, and it was said that a Spanish pilot had boasted that merchants and priests represented the first step toward the conquest of Japan. Sporadic persecutions continued until 1614, when Tokugawa Ieyasu began a serious movement to extirpate the foreign religion. Faced with torture, some Christians recanted. More than 3000 others were martyred.

The last resistance was an uprising near Nagasaki in 1637 and 1638 in which 37,000 Christians died. After that, Christianity survived in Japan only as a hidden religion with secret rites, with devotions to "Maria-Kannon," the mother of Jesus in the guise of the Buddhist goddess of mercy holding a child in her arms. A few of these "hidden Christians" reemerged in the late 19th century. Otherwise, apart from muskets and techniques of castle building, all that remained of the Portuguese influence were certain loan words that became a permanent part of the Japanese language: *pan* for bread, *birodo* for velvet, *shabon* for soap, *karuta* for playing cards, and *tempura* for that familiar Japanese dish.

Warring States and Era of Unification (1467–1600)	
1467–1568	Battles throughout Japan
1543	Portuguese arrive in Japan
1568	Oda Nobunaga takes Kyoto and partially unifies Japan
1575	Battle of Nagashino with spears and guns
1582	Nobunaga assassinated
1588	Hideyoshi sword hunt
1590	Hideyoshi completes unification
1592, 1597–8	Hideyoshi sends armies to Korea
1597	Hideyoshi bans Christianity
1598	Hideyoshi dies; his generals battle
1600	Tokugawa victory in Battle of Sekigahara, Ieyasu reunifies Japan

MEDIEVAL JAPAN IN HISTORICAL PERSPECTIVE

The term "feudal," as noted earlier, applies only loosely to Kamakura society: the Minamoto vassals were too few in number; the court government in Kyoto and its provincial and local offices were still functioning; and the Kyoto "establishment" of imperial family, nobles, and temples continued to own, manage, and receive income from their extensive estates. But most of these conditions had changed by the mid-16th century. The military class was larger; warrior fiefs had replaced estates; unigeniture had been established; the highest-ranking retainers of a *daimyo* held fiefs and vassals of their own; the economy and society had been totally revamped to meet the needs of the new rulers; and the warrior ethic was stronger than ever. In these respects Japan had indeed become feudal.

In other respects, however, Japan resembled postfeudal Europe. First, most of the military class were foot soldiers, not mounted warriors. They were called samurai and were vassals of a lord, but they were hardly feudal aristocrats in any sense of the term. They were not given fiefs but were paid with stipends of so many bales of rice. Second, unlike, say, medieval England, where the military class was about one quarter of one percent of the population, in mid-16th century Japan it may have reached seven or eight percent. It was more of a size with the mercenary armies of Europe during the 15th and 16th centuries. Third, the recruitment of village warriors added significantly to the power of Warring States daimyo but gave rise to problems as well. Taxes became harder to collect. Local samurai were often involved in uprisings. When organized by Pure Land Buddhist congregations, these uprisings sometimes involved whole provinces. Again, the parallels with postfeudal Europe seem closer. Fourth, even in a feudal society, not everything is feudal. The commercial growth of the Kamakura and Ashikaga periods continued through the dark decades of the Warring States era.

REVIEW QUESTIONS

1. Is there such a thing as an "aristocratic" culture, or does the term have no fixed content? Were Heian nobles more, or less, aristocratic than early Ashikaga warriors?

2. In the evolution of Japan's military class from the 10th to the 16h cenutry, what were the important turning points?

3. Contrast the high culture of the Ashikaga era with that of the late Heian period. Apart from becoming more military, how did it change?

4. What were the political and social consequences of Japan's wars after 1467?

SUGGESTED READINGS

P. J. ARNESON, *The Medieval Japanese* Daimyo: The *Ōuchi Family's Rule of Suō and Nagato* (1979). A sound account of the Warring States *daimyo.*

M. E. BERRY, *The Culture of Civil War in Kyoto* (1994). An insightful study of Kyoto in the 15th and 16th centuries.

M. E. BERRY, *Hideyoshi* (1982). A study of the 16th-century unifier of Japan.

D. BROWN AND E. ISHIDA, eds., *The Future and the Past* (1979). A translation of a history of Japan written in 1219.

M. COLLCUTT, *Five Mountains* (1980). A study of the monastic organization of medieval Zen.

P. DUUS, *Feudalism in Japan* (1969). An easy-to-read survey of the subject.

A. E. GOBLE, *Go-Daigo's Revolution* (1996). A provocative account of the 1331 revolt by an emperor who thought emperors should rule.

J. W. HALL AND J. P. MASS, eds., *Medieval Japan* (1974). A collection of topical essays on medieval history.

J. W. HALL, K. NAGAHARA, AND K. YAMAMURA, eds., *Japan Before Tokugawa* (1981). Another collection of essays on medieval history.

J. W. HALL AND T. TOYODA, *Japan in the Muromachi Age* (1977). Still another.

KEENE, ed., *Twenty Plays of the No Theatre* (1970). Medieval dramas. Wonderful cultural materials.

J. P. MASS, *The Development of Kamakura Rule, 1180–1250* (1979). Dry but detailed.

J. P. MASS AND W. HAUSER, eds., *The Bakufu in Japanese History* (1985). Topics in *bakufu* history from the 12th to the 19th centuries. Multi-author.

N. MCMULLIN, *Buddhism and the State in Sixteenth Century Japan* (1984) Nobunaga and his religious policies.

J. Piggott, *The Emergence of Japanese Kingship* (1997).

H. Sato, *Legends of the Samurai* (1995). Excerpts from various tales and writings.

C. Steenstrup, *Hōjō Shigetoki (1198–1261) and His Role in the History of Political and Ethical Ideas in Japan.* An important figure in the Hōjō rule of the late Kamakura period.

D. T. Suzuki, *Zen and Japanese Culture* (1959).

H. Tonomura, *Community and Commerce in Late Medieval Japan: The Corporate Villages of Tokuchin-ho* (1992). On a village during the Kamakura and Ashikaga eras.

H. P. Varley, *Imperial Restoration in Medieval Japan* (1971). A study of the 1331 attempt by an emperor to restore imperial power.

H. P. Varley, *The Ōnin War: History of Its Origins and Background with a Selective Translation of the Chronicle of Ōnin* (1967).

A. Waley, trans., *The Nō Plays of Japan* (1957). More wonderful medieval dramas.

K. Yamamura, ed., Vol. 5 of the *Cambridge History of Japan: Medieval Japan* (1990). Chapters by many leading scholars.

The commercial district of Osaka, the "kitchen" of Tokugawa Japan. Warehouses bear the crests of their merchant houses. Ships (upper right) loaded with rice, cotton goods, *sake*, and other goods are about to depart for Edo (Tokyo). Their captains vied with one another to arrive first and get the best price. [Courtesy A. Craig]

chapter three

The Era of Tokugawa Rule, 1600–1868

CHAPTER OUTLINE

In medieval Europe several countries went through a phase of "feudal monarchy." This rested on a balance between the center and outlying areas, an equilibrium in which all regional lords, while vassals of the king, were nonetheless largely autonomous in the management of their domains. But it was not a stable arrangement. In France, under successive monarchs, the country moved toward ever greater centralization until eventually the feudal lords lost their autonomy or were destroyed. In Germany, in contrast, the center lost out and many large and small states emerged. In terms of these European patterns, Tokugawa Japan is anomalous in that the equilibrium between a strong center and many semi-autonomous daimyo states did not break down but lasted for more than two centuries. This was due to Japan's isolation: the country was never seriously challenged by an external enemy. It was also due to the care with which the early Tokugawa leaders built the system.

POLITICAL UNIFICATION

The final years of the 16th century saw the culmination of trends that had begun a century earlier. By 1568 Oda Nobunaga (1534–1582) had conquered all of central Honshu. To promote the economy of this commercial heartland, he abolished guild monopolies and customs barriers. This economic unification, according to several historians, provided a base for political unification. But before Nobunaga could complete his conquests of the rest of Japan, he was assassinated in 1582 by a treacherous vassal. Another of his former vassals, Toyotomi Hideyoshi, who had begun his military career as a lowly foot soldier, completed the unification in 1590.

One problem of the peace that followed was the restive energies of his soldiers who knew only war. To deal with this, Hideyoshi decided to conquer China. In 1592 he sent an army of 160,000—a smaller force than the army of 280,000 he had used in Kyushu six years earlier—to Korea. The army quickly overran Korea but was forced to withdraw to the south when China sent its own army to rescue its "younger brother" state. Hideyoshi launched another attack in 1597, but he died the following year and the armies returned home.

Another problem was the existence of an armed peasantry. In war, village warriors fought for their lord; the strength they lent to his army was greater than the risk of their occasional uprisings. In peace only the risk remained. Accordingly, in the summer of 1588 Hideyoshi ordered a "sword hunt" to disarm the villagers. Records of the weaponry collected exist for only one county of 3400 households in Kaga, a domain on the Sea of Japan: 1,073 swords, 1,540 short swords, 700 daggers, 160 spears, 500 suits of armor, and other miscellaneous items. Once the hunt was completed, the 5 percent of the population who remained as castletown samurai used its monopoly on weapons to control the other 95 percent.

Hideyoshi next moved to freeze the social classes. Samurai were prohibited from quitting the service of their lord. Peasants were barred from abandoning their fields to become townspeople. Townspeople were prohibited from owning land. This policy was continued by the Tokugawa after 1600 and, by and large, succeeded—though with some blurring at class boundaries. Samurai, peasants, and townspeople tended to marry within their respective classes, and each class developed a unique cultural character. The authorities even attempted to dictate lifestyles, prescribing who could ride in palanquins, who could wear silk, and who was permitted to build fancy gates in front of their houses.

But to grasp the class structure of Tokugawa society, we must note the vast range of social gradations within each class. A farmer who was a landlord and district official was a more important figure than most lower samurai and lived in a different social world from a landless "water-drinking" peasant too poor to buy tea. A townsman could be the head of a great wholesale house, or a humble street peddler or clog mender. A samurai could be an elder—a key decision maker of his domain, with an income of thousands of bushels of rice and several hundred vassals of his own, or an impecunious foot soldier who stood guard at the castle gate.

Having disarmed the peasantry, Hideyoshi ordered cadastral surveys on his own lands and on those of his vassals. The surveys identified each parcel of land by location, size, soil quality, product, and cultivator's name. For the first time, an attempt was made to standardize the rods used to measure land and the boxes used to measure rice. These standards marked the beginning of the detailed recordkeeping that characterized the Tokugawa tax system. Based on these surveys, domains and fiefs were henceforth ranked in terms of their assessed yield.

POLITICAL ENGINEERING AND ECONOMIC GROWTH DURING THE SEVENTEENTH CENTURY

Even after reunification in 1600, the habits of mind of the Warring States era continued for a time. But with peace the character of the age slowly changed. To make their rule secure, Tokugawa leaders radically reshaped their society and political system. Vigorous economic and demographic growth also occurred. This combination of political and economic change made this a century of great dynamism.

Ieyasu and the Establishment of Tokugawa Rule

Bedazzled by his power and military successes, and against all the evidence of Warring States political behavior, Hideyoshi assumed that his vassals, governing as a collegial body, would honor their sworn oaths of loyalty to his heir. He was especially trustful of his great vassal Tokugawa Ieyasu (1542–1616), whose domains were larger than his own. His trust was misplaced. After his death in 1598, Hideyoshi's former vassals, paying little attention to his young heir, broke apart into two opposing camps and fought a great battle at Sekigahara in 1600 from which the alliance headed by Tokugawa Ieyasu emerged victorious. Ieyasu was wily and astute, skilled in managing his generals, a master strategist, and above all patient. In comparing the three unifiers, Japanese tell the story that when a cuckoo failed to sing, Nobunaga said, "I'll kill it if it doesn't sing"; Hideyoshi said," I'll make it sing"; but Ieyasu sat down and said, "I'll wait until it sings."

Like the Minamoto of 12th-century Kamakura, Ieyasu spurned the Kyoto court and established his headquarters in Edo (today's Tokyo) in the center of his military holdings in eastern Japan (see Map 3-1). He took the title of shogun in 1603 and called his government the *bakufu*. In Edo he built a great castle, surrounded by massive fortifications of stone and concentric moats. The inner portion of these moats and stone walls remains today as the Imperial Palace. Ieyasu then used his military power to reorganize Japan.

Ieyasu's first move was to confiscate the lands of his defeated enemies and to reward his vassals and allies. During the first quarter of the 17th century, the *bakufu* confiscated the domains of 150 daimyo: some of former enemies and some for infractions of the Tokugawa legal code; he then transferred 229 daimyo from one domain to another. The transfers completed the work of Hideyoshi's sword hunt by severing long-standing ties between daimyo and their former village retainers. When a daimyo was transferred to a new fief, he took his samurai retainers with him. During the second quarter of the 17th century, transfers and confiscations ended and the system settled down with a total of about 270 domains.

The reshuffling of domains had not been random. The configuration that emerged was, first, of a huge central Tokugawa domain. It contained the following: most of the domains of "house daimyo"—those who had been Tokugawa vassals before 1600; the fiefs of the 5000 Tokugawa bannermen (upper samurai); and the lands that furnished the stipends of the other 17,000 Tokugawa direct retainers (middle and lower samurai). Strategically placed around the Tokugawa heartland were the domains of the "related daimyo." Founded for the second and third sons of early shogun, these domains furnished successors to the main Tokugawa house when a

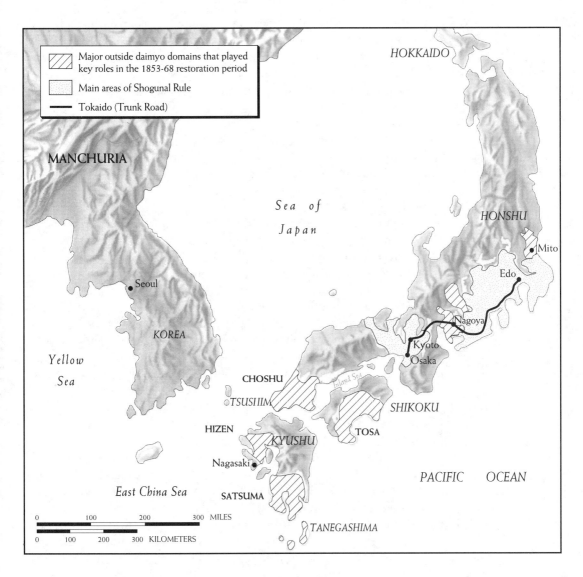

Map 3-1 Tokugawa Japan and the Korean peninsula.   The area between Edo and Osaka in central Honshu was both the political base of the Tokugawa *bakufu* and its rice basket. The domains that would overthrow the Tokugawa *bakufu* in the mid-nineteenth century were mostly in outlying areas of southwestern Japan.

shogun had no heir. Beyond the related daimyo was a second tier of "outside daimyo" who had fought as allies of Tokugawa Ieyasu in 1600 but became his vassals only after the battle was over.

Finally, at the antipodes of the system were the outside daimyo who had been permitted to survive despite having fought against the Tokugawa in 1600. Their domains were drastically reduced. They remained the "enemies" within the system, although they had submitted and become Tokugawa vassals soon after 1600. Thus, the entire arrangement constituted a defensive system, with the staunchest Tokugawa supporters nearest to Edo.

The Tokugawa also established other systemic controls: legal codes regulated the imperial court, temples and shrines, and daimyo; military houses were enjoined to employ vassals of ability and to practice frugality; daimyo were prohibited from engaging in drinking parties, wanton revelry, sexual indulgence, habitual gambling, or the ostentatious display of wealth. Only with *bakufu* consent could daimyo marry or repair their castles.

A second control was a hostage system, firmly established by 1642, that required the wives and children of daimyo to reside permanently in Edo and the daimyo to spend every second year in Edo. Like the policy of Louis XIV (r. 1643–1715) at Versailles, it transformed warrior lords into courtiers. The spacious Edo compounds of the daimyo contained hundreds or thousands of retainers and servants and occupied much of the city.

A third key control, established during the 1630s, was the national policy of seclusion. Seclusion was no barrier to cultural imports from China and Korea. But except for small Chinese and Dutch trading contingents at Nagasaki, no foreigners were permitted to enter Japan, and on pain of death, no Japanese were allowed to go abroad. Nor could ocean-going ships be built. The policy of seclusion was strictly enforced until 1854. Like the case of a watch, seclusion enclosed the workings of the entire system. Cut off from substantial outside political contacts, for Japanese, Japan became the world.

What, then, preserved the equilibrium between the *bakufu* and daimyo domains for over 250 years? Each side had strengths. The governments of the daimyo domains, like miniature *bakufu*, were staffed by their samurai vassals. High-ranking vassals held the higher offices. Each domain had its own autonomous military, finances, judiciary, schools, paper money, and so on. Because daimyo were vassals of the shogun, he could not easily move against them. The *bakufu* also had strengths: in addition to governing its own superdomain, it administered the controls over the whole system. Its offices were staffed by its vassals—its highest councils by house daimyo and high-ranking bannermen, and lesser posts by lower-ranking vassals of ability. The pool of rank was always larger than that of the available posts.

Within this equilibrium, it was critical that the governing councils of the *bakufu* were composed of house daimyo, the highest-ranking "old" vassals of the Tokugawa. Mostly from small domains, they were dedicated to maintaining the Tokugawa hegemony over big daimyo, but being daimyo themselves, they were careful to avoid policies that would curtail daimyo power. For example, they never established "royal courts" with jurisdiction over domain samurai, for that would have diminished their judicial powers within their own domains.

Economy and Society

The political dynamism of the period from Hideyoshi through the first century of Tokugawa rule was matched by dynamic economic growth. By the late 16th century, there existed a backlog of agricultural techniques, the spread of which had been impeded by regionalism and wars: methods of water control and irrigation that made double-cropping easier; better tools; new seed strains; the use of bony fish or night soil as fertilizers; and so on. During the 17th century these techniques were widely utilized. Resources no longer needed for war were allocated to land reclamation. The result was a doubling of agricultural production as well as a doubling of population, from 12 million in 1600 to 24 million in 1700. The production of agricultural byproducts—cotton, silk, indigo, lumber, dyes, and *sake*, and so on—also grew, especially in central Japan and along the shores of the Inland Sea.

Peace also sustained growth in commerce. The merchants in Warring States Japan, like geese who lay golden eggs, had always been at risk. They had to pay for security; they operated within cramped regional economies. On coming to power, Nobunaga and Hideyoshi were aware that political unification alone was not enough. They recognized that prosperity would make their rule easier and, acknowledging the enterprise of merchants, they abolished the medieval guilds and freed Japan's central markets from monopolistic restrictions. The result was a burgeoning of trade and the formation of a national market network atop the domain economies. As the network expanded during the 17th century, economic functions became more differentiated and efficient. The economic chain that began with a local buyer might extend to a merchant house in a regional port, to coastal shippers, to warehousers in Osaka or Edo, and then to great wholesale houses.

Seclusion ended much foreign trade. One might expect the decline in trade to have dampened Japan's domestic economy. Instead, commerce continued to grow for the remainder of the 17th century.

To explain this growth, we must look at the tax system and the pattern of consumption in the castletowns and Edo. Tokugawa taxes were based on land, not commerce. Taxes took about one third of a peasant's production. It was a heavier tax rate than that in China and bespeaks the effective rule of the military class. Most taxes were paid in rice. Even as late as the mid-19th century, only one third was collected in money payments. Thus, the 87 percent of the population who lived in the countryside paid almost one third of the country's agricultural wealth to the 5 percent in the military class. The remaining 8 percent of townspeople also lived off the tax flow by providing goods and services for samurai. This distribution of benefits was mirrored in the three-area city planning common to all castletowns: a large parklike area with castle, trees, stone walls, and moats for the daimyo and his government; extensive samurai quarters; and a meaner townspeople's quarter.

Moreover, just as the castletowns were the consumption centers of the regional tax economies, so was Edo the national consumption center and a super castletown. It had the same three-area layout, although on a far grander scale. When the daimyo of Kaga, from a great domain on the Japan Sea, was in attendance at Edo, he was served by 8000 samurai. When he returned to his domain, 4000 stayed on in Edo to manage the domain estates: 267 acres of houses and gardens, barracks, schools, warehouses, and so on. One of these estates, with its magnificent red gate still intact, is today the main campus of Tokyo University. Other daimyo had establishments proportional to their domains. By 1700 Edo had a population of about one million.

To support their Edo establishments, the daimyo sold tax rice in Osaka. Called the "kitchen of Japan," Osaka became the redistribution center from which competing fleets of coastal shippers brought food, clothing, lumber, oil, and other supplies to Edo. By 1700 Osaka's population was about 400,000. Kyoto, rebuilt after its destruction in the early Warring States period, was almost as big.

The bridal procession of Yohime, the twenty-first daughter of the eleventh Tokugawa shōgun, approaches the Edo mansion of the Kaga daimyo. The red gate (upper right), built in 1827 for this occasion, is today an entrance to the main campus of Tokyo University. The eleventh shōgun had twenty-eight sons and twenty-seven daughters by his more than forty concubines. Of his children, thirteen sons and twelve daughters survived to maturity. This woodblock print by Kunisada is a "national treasure." [Courtesy A. Craig]

It continued as a center of handicraft production. It was also the location of the "captive" imperial court, which, after suffering penury during the Warring States era, was given support lands equivalent in revenues to those of a small daimyo.

The system of alternate-year attendance at Edo contributed to the development of overland transportation. The most traveled grand trunk road was the *Tōkaidō* between Edo and Kyoto. The artist Hiroshige (1797–1858) made a series of wood-block prints that depicted the scenery at its 53 post stations. The stations had official inns for traveling daimyo and requisitioned supplies and horses as a tax on adjacent villages. These stations often grew into thriving local towns.

The growth of a national economy led to a richness and diversity in urban life. Townsmen governed their districts. Samurai magistrates watched over the city as a whole. Public services were provided by schools, police, and companies of fire-fighters—a proverb of the time was "fires are the flowers of Edo." But there were also servants, cooks, messengers, restaurant owners, priests, doctors, teachers, sword sharpeners, book lenders, instructors in the martial arts, geisha, prostitutes, and bath-house attendants. In the world of the popular arts, there were woodblock printers and artists, book publishers, puppeteers, acrobatic troupes, storytellers, and Kabuki and Nō actors. Merchant establishments included money changers, pawnbrokers, small shops, single-price retail establishments like the House of Mitsui, and great wholesale merchants. Merchant households furnished the raw materials for the personae of Edo fiction: the skinflint merchant who pinches every penny, the profligate son who runs through an inheritance to an inevitable bankruptcy, an erring wife, or the clerk involved in a hopeless affair with a prostitute.

THE EIGHTEENTH AND EARLY NINETEENTH CENTURIES

By the late 17th century, the political reengineering of the Tokugawa state was complete. After that, few major new laws were enacted, and few important changes were made in governing institutions. In the economy, too, from the early 18th century, dynamic growth gave way to slower growth within a high-level equilibrium. In the words of some historians, the society had become "frozen," "unchanging," or "strangely preserved." Yet changes of a different kind were underway.

The Forty-Seven Rōnin

The 18th century began with high drama. In the spring of 1701 a daimyo on duty at Edo Castle drew his sword and slightly wounded a *bakufu* official who had insulted him. Even to unsheath a sword within the castle was punishable by death.

The Virtuous Wife

The three-generation stem family, composed of the older parents, their eldest son and his "bride," and their children, was the ideal during the Edo period. The principal family bond was between the parents and their elder son. The son's "bride," at least until she produced children of her own, was less than a full family member, as is suggested in the adage "the womb is borrowed." Kaibara Ekken (1630–1714), an early Confucian moralist, propounded an ethic appropriate to such a family in his *Greater Learning for Women*. It reflects the "wisdom" of his age.

Can any ethic that serves a society be accepted and practiced? Or, are some ethics more "natural" than others? How did a girl raised in Tokugawa society feel? Could she embrace Ekken's teachings? Or, does the following passage suggest, at least obliquely, that some human feelings are universal and difficult to deny?

GIRL'S INSTRUCTION

Seeing that it is a girl's destiny, on reaching womanhood, to go to a new home, and live in submission to her father-in-law, it is even more incumbent upon her than it is on a boy to receive with all reverence her parents' instructions. Should her parents, through her tenderness, allow her to grow up self-willed, she will infallibly show herself capricious in her husband's house, and thus alienate his affection; while, if her father-in-law be a man of correct principles, the girl will find the yoke of these principles intolerable. She will hate and decry her father-in-law, and the end of these domestic dissensions will be her dismissal from her husband's house and the covering of herself with ignominy. Her parents, forgetting the faulty education they gave her, may, indeed, lay all the blame on the father-in-law. But they will be in error; for the whole disaster

On the same day, the daimyo was ordered to commit *harakiri* (literally, to cut his stomach), and his domain was confiscated. Fearing an attempt at revenge, the *bakufu* police kept an eye on the daimyo's retainers—now *rōnin*, or "masterless samurai." The retainers dissembled, working at lowly jobs, staying at home with their families, or leading lives of drunkenness and debauchery.

Twenty-one months later, on a snowy night in January, 47 of the retainers gathered in Edo, attacked the residence of the *bakufu* official, took his head, and then surrendered to the authorities. Their act stirred the imagination of the citizenry of Edo and was widely acclaimed. But the *bakufu* council, after deliberating for two months, ordered all 47 to commit *harakiri*. Embodying as it did the perennial theme of duty versus human feelings, the incident was quickly taken up by writers of Kabuki drama and puppet theater; to this day it has been reworked into novels, movies, and televi-

should rightly be attributed to the faulty education the girl received from her parents.

THE INFIRMITIES OF WOMAN

The five worst infirmities that afflict the female are indocility, discontent, slander, jealousy, and silliness. Without any doubt, these five infirmities are found in seven or eight out of every ten women, and it is from these that arises the inferiority of women to men. A woman should cure them by self-inspection and self-reproach.

THE WIFE'S MISCELLANEOUS DUTIES

A woman has no particular lord. She must look to her husband as her lord, and must serve him with all worship and reverence, not despising or thinking lightly of him. The great lifelong duty of a woman is obedience. In her dealings with her husband, both the expresesion of her countenance and style of her address should be courteous, humble, and concil-iatory, never peevish and intractable, never rude and arrogant—that should be a woman's first and chiefest care. When the husband issues his instructions, the wife must never disobey them. In doubtful cases she should inquire of her husband, and obediently follow his commands. If ever her husband should inquire of her, she should answer to the point—to answer in a careless fashion would be a mark of rudeness. Should her husband be roused at any time to anger, she must obey him with fear and trembling, and not set herself up against him in anger and forwardness. A woman should look on her husband as if he were Heaven itself, and never weary of thinking how she may yield to her husband and thus escape celestial castigation.

Kaibara Ekken, *Greater Learning for Women* in K. Hoshino, *The Way of Contentment* (London: John Murray, © 1913, reprinted 1979), pp. 33–34, 44–45.

sion scripts. Just as Western theater has had many different Hamlets, so have there been many characterizations of Ōishi Kuranosuke, the leader of the band of 47.

Viewed historically, three points may be noted about the incident. First, in a similar situation, the more realistic samurai of the Warring States period would have forgotten their former lord and rushed to find a new one. Loyalty was highly valued because disloyalty was a live option. But this was no longer true in the Tokugawa era. With the authority of the daimyo backed by that of the shogun, there was no room for disloyalty. So loyalty became deeply internalized and was viewed almost as a religious obligation. Also, it was easier for Tokugawa samurai to be loyal unto death because, for the most part, there was so little likelihood in an era of peace that such a loyalty would be called for. In any case, in 1701 it was this Tokugawa species of absolute loyalty that moved the 47 ronin.

Talent and Rule

From ancient times, Confucian philosophers were divided. Some felt that human nature was good and that the social order should be grounded in that goodness. Others felt that human nature was wayward and that only firm institutions and rules of behavior could ensure an orderly society. Ogyū Sorai (1666–1728) was the foremost Tokugawa advocate of the latter position and advocated, accordingly, strong laws and institutions. But who should operate these institutions? Sorai seemed to equivocate. On the one hand, he favored a hereditary ruling class of military households. On the other hand, he believed that hereditary rule would engender bad government and lead, ultimately, to the collapse of the regime.

Is Sorai predicting the collapse of the Tokugawa order? Or is he advocating a limited and selective use of men of talent, such as himself, to maintain the system in good order? Was the durability of Tokugawa institutions due to its use of talent?

Why is it that during a period of prolonged peace men of ability are only found among the lower classes, while men of the upper class grow increasingly stupid? As far as I can see, men's abilities are developed only through hardship and tribulation. In the case of our bodies, use makes the members strong. Use the hands and the arms grow strong, use the legs and the feet become hardened. If one practices aiming as in archery or gunnery, one's eyesight will improve. Likewise, when the mind is used, intelligence develops. If hardship and tribulation are encountered in different forms, these experiences will bring out one's abilities; that is the natural law. So in Mencius it

Second, the incident tells something of the state in Tokugawa Japan. The 1615 "Laws for the Military Houses" contained the passage. "Law is the basis of the social order. Reason may be violated in the name of law, but law may not be violated in the name of reason. Those who break laws deserve heavy punishments."[1] One Tokugawa law explicitly forbade private vendettas. So, despite the moral purity of their act—which was recognized by all, even by those who condemned them to death—the 47 "virtuous warriors" had to die. The state was above ethics. The death sentence was a bureaucratic necessity.

Third, loyalty and idealism were not a monopoly of samurai males. In the dramatized versions, at least, samurai wives and daughters, and merchants, too, displayed the same heroic spirit of self-sacrifice.

[1] R. Tsunoda, W.T. de Bary, and D. Keene, eds., *Sources of the Japanese Tradition* (New York: Columbia University Press, 1958), p. 336.

is noted that when Heaven has a great mission for a man to perform, it will first put him to an acid test. When he develops his ability through such a acid test, he is especially fit for the task of government because he is familiar with conditions among the people. Therefore, in the Way of the Sages too, it is recommended that able men be advanced by bringing them up from below. Through the study of history also we may see, as clearly as in a mirror, that men of intelligence and talent have all come from below; rarely have they come from hereditarily privileged families. Even those men of the hereditary nobility have come to that high estate because their forebears risked their lives during the Warring States period, developed their abilities the hard way through bitter experience, and rendered distinguished service in order to attain high office and large feudal grants. Their descendants, however, having held high office and large feudal grants for generations, find themselves on top from birth and suffer no hardship at all. How then can they develop their abilities? Set apart from those below by their high rank, they are uninformed of conditions among the people. Brought up amidst the constant flattery of those around them, they pride themselves on their wisdom without in truth having any . . .

Such is human nature, the same in the present as in the past. For this reason, in the Way of the Sages, prime importance was placed on raising up wise and talented men of low station, while hereditary succession in high office from generation to generation was strongly disapproved.

R. Tsunoda, W. T. de Bary, and D. Keene, eds., *Sources of the Japanese Tradition* (New York: Columbia University Press, © 1958), pp. 432–433. Reprinted with permission of the publisher.

Cycles of Reform

Most political history of late Tokugawa Japan is written in terms of alternating cycles of laxity and reform. Even during the mid-17th century the expenses of the *bakufu* and daimyo states were often greater than their income. In part, the reason was structural: taxes were based on agriculture in an economy that was becoming commercial. In part, it was simple mathematics: after the samurai were paid their yearly stipends, not enough was left for the expenses of domain governments and the upkeep of the Edo establishments. In part, it was the toll of extraordinary costs, such as a *bakufu* levy, the wedding of a daimyo's daughter, or the rebuilding of a castle after a fire. And finally, in part, it was a growing taste for luxury among daimyo and their retainers of rank.

Over the years, a familiar pattern emerged. To make ends meet, domains would borrow from merchants. Then, as finances became even more straitened, a reformist clique of officials would appear, gain power, retrench the domain's finances, eliminate extravagance, and return the domain to a more frugal and austere way of life. Debts would be repaid or repudiated. A side effect of reform was the depression of the local merchant economy. But no one likes to practice frugality forever. So, after some goals of the reform had been achieved, a new clique would take over the government and a new round of spending would begin. The *bakufu* carried out three major reforms on the lands it controlled directly:

1716–1733	Tokugawa Yoshimune	17 years
1787–1793	Matsudaira Sadanobu	6 years
1841–1843	Mizuno Tadakuni	2 years

The first two, done by shogun, were long and successful; the third was not. Its failure set the stage for the ineffective response of the *bakufu* to the West in the mid-19th century. Reforms were also carried out by daimyo domains. Some were successful, enabling them to respond more effectively to the political crisis of the mid-19th century.

Bureaucratization

The balance between centralization and decentralization lasted until the end of the Tokugawa era. Not a single domain attempted to overthrow the *bakufu* hegemony. Nor did the *bakufu* ever try to extend its control over the domains. But bureaucracy grew steadily within the *bakufu* and within each domain. One development was the extension of public authority into areas that had been private. In 1600 most samurai fiefs were run by their samurai fief holders. The samurai collected the taxes, often at a heavier rate than that set by the domain, and appointed fief stewards to oversee the fiefs. By 1850, however, all but the largest of samurai fiefs were administered by district officials. They collected the standard domain taxes and forwarded to the samurai their income. In periods of retrenchment, samurai were often paid only half the amount due.

Along with the growth in bureaucracy was the proliferation of administrative codes and government by paperwork. Surviving domain archives house room after room of records of every imaginable kind, mostly from the late 18th and early 19th centuries: records of births, adoptions, name changes, samurai ranks, fiefs, stipends, land holdings, taxes, court proceedings, domain history, and so on. Administrative codes for the *bakufu* exchequer, for example, grew from a single page during the 17th century to 40 pages in the late Tokugawa. They define, among other things, an elaborate structure of offices and suboffices, their jurisdictional boundaries, and detailed instructions as to how many copies of each document should be made and to which offices they should be forwarded.

Of course, there were limits to bureaucratization. Only samurai could aspire to official posts. They came to the office wearing their two swords and formal dress.

Decision-making posts were limited to upper-ranking samurai. In periods of financial crises—endemic in the late Tokugawa—a demand arose for men of ability, and middle-or lower-middle-ranking samurai joined domain decision-making by becoming staff assistants to bureaucrats of rank.

The Later Tokugawa Economy

By 1700 the economy had approached the limit of expansion within the available technology. The population, an important index, reached 26 million early in the 18th century and was at the same figure in the mid-19th century, a period during which the population of China more than doubled. Within this constant figure were various smaller movements. Population declined during epidemics in the 1750s and the 1760s and during famines in the 1780s. The northeast never fully recovered. Southwestern Japan along the Inland Sea gained in population. Central Japan stayed even; it was more urban, and like most premodern cities, Tokugawa cities had higher death rates.

After 1700, taxes stabilized and land surveys were few. Evidence suggests little increase in grain production and only slow growth in agricultural byproducts. Some families made conscious efforts to limit family size in order to raise their standard of living. Contraception and abortion were commonplace, and infanticide (euphemistically called *mabiki*, the term for thinning out rice shoots in a paddy) was practiced in hard times. But disease, periodic shortages of food, and late marriages among the poor were more important factors. A study of one rural village showed the daughters of poor farmers marrying at 22 and having an average of 4.6 children, whereas for the daughters of rich farmers the figures were 19 and 6.2. A study of another domain showed a decline in the size of the average farm household from 7 to 4.25 members.

During the Tokugawa some farmers remained independent, small cultivators, but others became landlords or tenants. About a quarter of all cultivated lands was worked by tenants by the mid-19th century. Most landlords were small, lived in their villages, and often were village leaders. They were not at all like the Chinese gentry. The misery of the lower stratum of rural society contributed to an increase in peasant uprisings during the late 18th and early 19th centuries. Authorities had no difficulty in quelling them, although a few involved thousands of protestors and were locally destructive. No uprising in Japan even remotely approached those of late Manchu China.

Commerce grew slowly during the late Tokugawa. Early in the 18th century, it was reencased within guilds. Merchants paid set fees, usually not especially high, in exchange for monopoly privileges in central marketplaces. Guilds were also reestablished in the domains, and some domains established domain-run monopolies on products such as wax, paper, indigo, or sugar. The problem facing domain leaders was how to tax profits without injuring the competitive standing of domain exports. Most late Tokugawa commercial growth was in countryside industries—*sake*, soy sauce, dyes, silks, or cotton—and was especially prominent in central and western Japan. Some were organized and financed by city merchants under the putting-out system. Others competed with city merchants, shipping directly to end markets to circumvent monopoly controls. The expansion of labor in such rural industries contributed to the population shrinkage in late Tokugawa cities.

The largest question about the Tokugawa economy concerns its relation to Japan's amazing industrialization in the late 19th century. Some scholars have suggested that Japan had a "running start." Others have stressed Japanese backwardness in comparison with European late developers. The question is still unresolved.

TOKUGAWA CULTURE

If the *Tale of Genji* represents the classical culture of the aristocratic Heian court, and if Nō drama or an ink painting by Sesshū represents the austere samurai culture of medieval Japan, then a satire by Saikaku (1642–1693), a drama by Chikamatsu (1653–1724), or a woodblock print of a beauty by Utamaro (1753–1806) may be taken to represent the new urban culture of the Tokugawa era. In such works one discerns a new secular consciousness, an exquisite taste put to plebeian ends, occasional vulgarities, and a sense of humor only occasionally found in the earlier tradition.

But there was more to Tokugawa culture than the arts and literature of the townspeople. Two hundred and fifty years of peace and prosperity provided a base for an ever more complex culture and a broader popular participation in cultural life. In villages Buddhism became more deeply rooted, new folk religions proliferated. By the early 19th century most well-to-do farmers could read and write. The aristocratic culture of the ranking samurai houses also remained vigorous. Nō plays continued to be staged. Chinese-style poems were written. The medieval tradition of black ink paintings was continued by the Kanō school and other artists.

The Ashikaga tradition of restraint, simplicity, and naturalness in architecture was extended. The imperial villa in Katsura on the outskirts of Kyoto has its roots in medieval architecture and to this day inspires Japanese architects. The gilded and colored screen paintings that had surged in popularity during Hideyoshi's rule developed further, culminating in the powerful works of Ogata Kōrin (1658–1716).

Zen Buddhism, having declined during the Warring States period, was revitalized by the monk Hakuin (1686–1769). One of the great cultural figures of the Tokugawa era, Hakuin was also a writer, painter, calligrapher, and sculptor. His autobiographical writings have been translated as *The Embossed Tea Kettle*.

Some scholars have argued that Tokugawa urban culture had a double structure. On the one hand were the samurai, serious and high-minded, who produced a vast body of Chinese-style paintings, poetry, and philosophical treatises. On the other hand was the culture of the townspeople: lowbrow, irreverent, sentimental, secular, satirical, and at times scatological. The samurai esteemed Sung-style paintings of mountains and waterfalls, often adorned with quotations from the Confucian classics or T'ang poetry. The townspeople collected prints of local beauties, actors, courtesans, and scenes of the

"Mother Bathing Her Son." Woodblock print by Kitagawa Utamaro (1753–1806). Note the cooper's craft seen in the tub, the wooden clog, the simple yet elegant kimono design, and a second kimono hanging to dry at the upper right corner. [Color woodblock print 14⅞″ × 10⅛″ (37.8 × 25.7 cm.). Photo: M. McLean The Nelson-Atkins Museum of Art, Kansas City, MO (Purchase: Nelson Trust). © The Nelson Gallery Foundation. All Reproduction Rights Reserved.]

hustle and bustle of everyday life. Samurai moralists saw money as the root of evil. Merchants saw it as their goal in life; in Osaka they even held an "abacus festival," at which they consecrated their adding machines to the gods of wealth and commerce.

In poetry, too, a double structure appeared. Bashō (1644–1694) was born a samurai but gave up his status to live as a wandering poet. He is famous for his travel journal, *The Narrow Road of Oku*, and for his *haiku*, little word–picture poems:

Such stillness—
The cries of the cicadas
Sink into the rocks.

A crow perches
On a leafless branch
An autumn evening.

On visiting the battlefield at Sekigahara where the Tokugawa vanquished their enemies, he mused

The summer grass
All that is left
Of a warrior's dream. [2]

Contrast Bashō's sense of the transience of life with the worldliness of the townsman:

From a mountain temple
The snores of a monk and
the voice of the cuckoo.

Showing a love letter
to her mother
From a man she doesn't love.

Even the most virtuous woman
will undo her sash
For a flea. [3]

This is not to say, of course, that townsmen did not also write proper *haiku*.

[2]D. Keene, ed., *Anthology of Japanese Literature* (New York: Grove Press, 1955), p. 371.
[3]R. H. Blyth, *Japanese Humor* (Tokyo: Japanese Travel Bureau, 1957), p. 141.

Tokugawa Era (1600–1868)

1600	Tokugawa Ieyasu reunifies Japan
1615	"Laws of Military Houses" issued
1639	Seclusion policy adopted
1642	Edo hostage system in place
1644–1694	Bashō, poet
1653–1724	Chikamatsu Monzaemon, dramatist
1701	The 47 rōnin avenge their lord
1853, 1854	Commodore Matthew Perry visits Japan

Literature and Drama

Is cultural creativity more likely during periods of economic growth and political change or during periods of stability? The greatest works of literature and philosophy of Tokugawa Japan were produced between 1650 and 1725, just as the initial political transformation was being completed but the economy still growing and the society not yet set in its ways.

One of the major literary figures and certainly the most entertaining was Ihara Saikaku (1642–1693), who is generally credited with having recreated the Japanese novel. Saikaku was heir to an Osaka merchant house. He was raised to be its master, but after his wife died, he let the head clerk manage the business and devoted himself to poetry, theater, and the pleasure quarters. At the age of 40, he wrote and illustrated *The Life of an Amorous Man*, the story of a modern and bawdy Prince Genji who cuts a swathe through bathhouse girls, shrine maidens, courtesans, and boy actors. The overnight success of the work led to a sequel, *The Life of an Amorous Woman*, the tale of a woman of good lineage undone by passion and of her downward spiral through the minutely graded circles of the Osaka demimonde. Saikaku also wrote more than 20 other works, including the *The Japanese Family Storehouse*, which humorously chronicles the contradictions between the pursuit of wealth and the pursuit of pleasure.

A second major figure of this Osaka culture at the turn of the century was the dramatist Chikamatsu Monzaemon (1653–1724). Born a samurai in Echizen province, Chikamatsu entered the service of a court noble in Kyoto and then, in 1705, moved to Osaka to write for both the Kabuki and puppet theater.

Kabuki had begun early in the 17th century as suggestive skits and erotic dances performed by troupes of itinerant actresses. In 1629 the *bakufu* forbade women to perform on the stage. By the 1660s Kabuki had evolved into a more serious drama with male actors playing both male and female roles. Actors entered the stage on a raised runway or "flower path" through the audience. Famous actors took great liberties in interpreting their roles, to roars of approval from the audience. There was a ready market for woodblock prints of actors in their most famous roles—like posters of rock musicians today but done with incomparably greater artistry.

The three main types of Kabuki plays were dance pieces, influenced by Nō; domestic dramas; and historical pieces. Chikamatsu wrote all three. In contrast to Saikaku's protagonists, the men and women in Chikamatsu's plays are torn between their human feelings and the duty to fulfill the obligations of their station in life. Only when their passions become uncontrollable, which is generally the case, do the plays end in tragedy. The emotional intensity of the ending is heightened by the restraint the actors show before reaching their breaking point. In several plays the hero and heroine leave duty behind and, hoping for felicity in the next world, set out on a flight to death. Another favorite ending is the double suicide, in which the thwarted lovers choose union in the next world. Indeed, this ending was banned by *bakufu* authorities when the excessive popularity of the drama led to its imitation in real life.

It is interesting to compare Kabuki and the Nō drama. Nō is like early Greek drama in that the chorus chants the narrative, to the accompaniment of flutes and drums. In Nō the stylization of action is extreme. In Kabuki, as in Elizabethan drama, the actors declaim their lines in the dramatic realism demanded by the commoner theatergoers of 17th-century Japan. But to convey the illusion of realism requires

One of Edo's three Kabuki theaters during the 1790s. The male actors provide the drama—even female roles are played by men. The audience eats, drinks, and smokes while watching the action. Note the mix of social classes: Day laborers at center-left sit on boards while well-to-do merchants occupy more expensive seats in the right and left foreground. At bottom-center an artisan cadges a light for his pipe. Several boxes to his left, another pours a drink. A reprint of a three-panel woodblock print by Utagawa Toyokuni (1769–1825) from the late 1970s. [Musee Guimet, Paris, France/Giraudon/Art Resource, N.Y.]

some deviation from it. As Chikamatsu noted about Kabuki, "Many things are said by the female characters which real women could not utter. . . . It is because they say what could not come from a real woman's lips that their true emotions are disclosed." For him, "Art is something that lies in the slender margin between the real and the unreal."[4] Yet, for all that Chikamatsu was concerned for the refinements of his craft and the subtle balance between emotional expressiveness and unspoken restraints, he never talked of the mysterious "no mind" as the key to an actor's power. His dramas are a world removed from the religiosity of the medieval Nō.

In the early 18th century Kabuki was displaced in popularity by the puppet theater (Bunraku). Many of Chikamatsu's plays were written for this genre. The word "puppet" does not do justice to the half-life-sized human figures, which rival Nō masks in their artistry. Manipulated by a team of three in black cloaks, a puppet does not only kneel and bow or engage in swordplay, but can also mimic brushing a tear from the eye or threading a needle. In the late 18th century the puppet theater, in turn, declined, and as the center of culture shifted from Osaka to Edo, Kabuki again blossomed as Japan's premier form of drama.

Confucian Thought

The most important change in Tokugawa intellectual life was the shift within the ruling elite from the religious worldview of Buddhist toward the more secular teachings of Confucius. The reworking occurred slowly. During the 17th century samurai were enjoined never to forget the arts of war and to be ever ready to die for their lord. One samurai in his deathbed poem lamented dying on *tatami*—with his boots off, as it were. At the time most samurai were illiterate and saw book learning as unmanly. Nakae Tōju (1608–1648), a samurai and a Confucian scholar, recounted that as a youth he swaggered around with his friends during the day and studied secretly at night so as not to be thought a sissy. Schools, too, were slow to develop. One Japanese scholar has noted that in 1687 only four domains had proper domain schools; in 1715, only ten.

The great figures of Tokugawa Confucianism lived during the same years as Saikaku and Chikamatsu, in the late 17th and early 18th centuries. They are great because they succeeded in the difficult task of adapting Chinese Confucianism to fit Japanese society. One problem, for example, was that in Chinese Confucianism there was no place for a shogun, whereas in the Japanese tradition of sun-line emperors, there was no room for the Mandate of Heaven. Most Tokugawa thinkers handled this discrepancy by saying that heaven gave the emperor its mandate to rule and that the emperor then entrusted political authority to the shogun. One philosopher suggested that the divine emperor acted for heaven and gave the mandate to the shogun. Neither solution was satisfactory, for, in fact, the emperor was as much a puppet as those in the Osaka theater.

[4]R. Tsunoda, pp. 447–448.

Sontoku's Pill

It is hard to imagine religious or philosophies more radically different than Shinto, with its host of amorphous, animistic nature deities; Buddhism, with its philosophy of transcendence and denial of this world; and Confucianism, with its this-worldly emphasis on ethics and good government. Yet in the Tokugawa era these not only coexisted but were commingled in the rituals and routines of daily life. Ninomiya Sontoku (1787–1856) was born a peasant and became a moralist, agrarian economist, planner, and local reformer. His ideas had sufficient force that they were revived and adapted for programs of rural reform during the 1920s and 1930s. In the following passage he addresses the issue of the "three religions."

What does Sontoku's rejection of "lofty speculation" suggest regarding Tokugawa thought? In our own modern society is the reconciliation of the unworldly (religious doctrines) and the worldly (science and material goals) basically different from that of Sontoku? If so, how?

Old Ninomiya once said, "I have long pondered about Shinto—what it calls the Way, what are its virtues and what its deficiencies; and about Confucianism—what its teaching consists in, what are its virtues and deficiencies; and also about Buddhism—what do its various sects stand for, and what are their virtues and deficiencies. And so I wrote a poem:

| Yo no naka wa | The things of this world |
| Sute ajirogi no | Are like lengths |

Another problem was the difference between China's centralized bureaucratic government and Japan's feudal system of lord–vassal relationships. Samurai loyalty was clearly not that of a scholar-official to the Chinese emperor. Some Japanese thinkers solved the problem rather ingeniously by saying that it was China that had deviated from the feudal society of the Chou sages, whereas in Japan, Tokugawa Ieyasu had recreated just such a society.

A third problem concerned the "central flowery kingdom" and the "barbarians" around it. No philosopher could quite bring himself to say that Japan was the real middle kingdom and China the barbarian, but some argued that centrality was relative, and still others suggested that China under barbarian Manchu rule had lost all claim to universality. These are just a few of a large range of problems related to Japanese political organization, family practices, and Shinto. By the early 18th century these problems had been addressed and a revised Confucianism acceptable for use in Japan had come into being.

Another point to note is the continuing vitality of Japanese thought—Confucian and otherwise—into the mid-19th century. This vitality is partly explained by the disputes among different schools of Confucianism and partly, perhaps, by Japan's lack of an examination system. The best energies of its samurai youth were not channeled into writing the conventional and sterile "eight-legged essays" that were required in

Take-kurabe	Of bamboo rod
Sore kore tomo ni	For use in fish nets—
Nagashi mijikashi	That one's too long,
	That one too short.

"Such was my dissatisfaction with them. Now let me state the strong and weak points of each. Shinto is the Way which provides the foundation of the country; Confucianism is the Way which provides for governing the country; and Buddhism is the Way which provides for governing one's mind. Caring no more for lofty speculation than for humble truth, I have tried simply to extract the essence of each of these teachings. By essence I mean their importance to mankind. Selecting what is important and discarding what is unimportant, I have arrived at the best teaching for mankind, which I call the teaching of Repaying Virtue. I also call it the 'pill containing the essence of Shinto, Confucianism and Buddhism.' " . . .

Kimigasa Hyōdayū asked the proportions of the prescription in this "pill," and the old man replied, "One spoon of Shinto, and a half-spoon each of Confucianism and Buddhism."

Then someone drew a circle, one half of which was marked Shinto and two quarter-segments labeled Confucianism and Buddhism respectively. "Is it like this?" he asked. The old man smiled, "You won't find medicine like that anywhere. In a real pill all the ingredients are thoroughly blended so as to be indistinguishable. Otherwise it would taste bad in the mouth and feel bad in the stomach."

R. Tsunoda, W. T. de Bary, and D. Keene, eds., *Sources of the Japanese Tradition* (New York: Columbia University Press, © 1990), pp. 584–585. Reprinted with permission of the publisher.

the Chinese examination system. Official preferment—within the constraints of Japan's hereditary system—was often obtained by writing a proposal for domain reforms, although this could lead to punishments as well.

The vitality was also a result of the rapid expansion of schools that began in the early 18th century. By the early 19th century, every domain had its own official school and another at its Edo estates. Commoner schools (*terakoya*), in which reading, writing, and the rudiments of Confucianism were taught, grew apace. In the first half of the 19th century private academies also appeared throughout the country. By the late Tokugawa era about 40 to 50 percent of the male and 15 to 20 percent of the female populations may have been literate—a far higher rate than in most of the world, and on a par with some European late developers.

Other Developments in Thought

For Tokugawa scholars, the problem of how to deal with China was vexing. Their response was usually ambivalent. They praised China as the teacher-country and respected its creative tradition. They studied its history, philosophy, and literature and began a tradition of scholarship on China that has remained powerful to this day. But they also sought to retain a separate Japanese identity. Most scholars dealt with this problem by adapting Confucianism to fit Japan. But two schools—never in the mainstream of Tokugawa thought, but of growing importance during the 18th and early 19th centuries—arrived at more radical positions. The schools of National Studies and Dutch Studies were diametrically opposed in most respects but alike in criticizing the Chinese influence on Japanese life and culture.

National Studies began as philological studies of ancient Japanese texts. One source of its inspiration was Shinto. Another was the Neo-Confucian school of Ancient Learning. Just as the School of Ancient Learning had sought to discover the original, true meanings of the Chinese classics before they were contaminated by Sung metaphysics, so the scholars in the National Studies tradition tried to find in the Japanese classics the original, true character of Japan before it had become contaminated by Chinese ideas. On studying the *Record of Ancient Matters*, the *Collection of Myriad Leaves*, or the *Tale of Genji*, they found that the early Japanese spirit was free, spontaneous, pure, lofty, and honest, in contrast to the Chinese spirit, which they characterized as rigid, cramped, and artificial. Some writings in this school appear to have borrowed the anti-Confucian logic of Taoism.

A second characteristic of National Studies was its proto-nationalistic affirmation of Shinto. Motoori Norinaga (1730–1801) wrote of Shinto creationism as the "Right Way":

> Heaven and Earth, all the gods and all phenomena, were brought into existence by the creative spirits of two deities. . . . This . . . is a miraculously divine act the reason for which is beyond the comprehension of the human intellect. . . .
>
> But in foreign countries where the Right Way has not been transmitted, this act of divine creativity is not known. Men there have tried to explain the principle of Heaven and earth and all phenomena by such theories as the yin and yang, the hexagrams of the Book of Changes, and the Five Elements. But all of these are fallacious theories stemming from the assumptions of the human intellect and they in no wise represent the true principle. . . .
>
> The "special dispensation of our Imperial Land" means that ours is the native land of the Heaven-Shining Goddess who casts her light over all countries in the four seas. Thus our country is the source and fountain-head of all other countries, and in all matters it excels all the others.[5]

National Studies became influential during the late Tokugawa era. It had a small but not unimportant influence on the Meiji Restoration. Its doctrines continued thereafter as one strain of modern Japanese ultranationalism. Its most enduring achievement was in Japanese linguistics. Even today, scholars admire Motoori's

---

[5]R. Tsunoda, pp. 521, 523.

philology. Moreover, in an age when the prestige of things Chinese was over-whelming, Motoori helped redress the balance by appreciating and giving a name to the aesthetic sensibility found in the Japanese classics. He called it *mono no aware*, which literally means "the poignancy of things."

But National Studies had weaknesses that prevented it from becoming the main-stream of Japanese thought. First, even the most refined sensibility is no substitute for philosophy. In its celebration of the primitive, National Studies ran headlong into the greater rationality of Confucian thought. Second, National Studies was chiefly literary, and apart from its enthusiasm for the divine emperor, it had little to offer in an age when political philosophy was central in both domain and *bakufu* schools.

The second development was Dutch Studies. After Christianity had been pro-scribed and the policy of seclusion adopted, all Western books were banned in Japan. Some knowledge of Dutch was maintained among the official interpreters who dealt with the Dutch at Nagasaki. The ban on Western books (except for those propagating Christianity) was ended in 1720 by the shogun Tokugawa Yoshimune (r. 1716–1745), fol-lowing the advice of a scholar whom he had appointed to reform the Japanese calendar.

During the remainder of the 18th century, a school of "Dutch medicine" became established in Japan. Japanese pioneers recognized early that Western anatomy texts were superior to Chinese. The first Japanese dissection of a corpse was performed in 1754. In 1774 a Dutch translation of a German anatomy text was trans-lated into Japanese. By the mid-19th century schools of Dutch Studies were to be found in the main cities of Japan, and instruction was available in some domains as well. Fukuzawa Yukichi (1835–1901), who studied Dutch and Dutch science during the mid-1850s at a school begun in 1838 in Osaka, wrote in his autobiography of the hostility of his fellow students toward Chinese learning:

> Though we often had discussions on many subjects, we seldom touched upon political subjects as most of us were students of medicine. Of course, we were all for free intercourse with Western countries, but there were few among us who took a serious interest in that problem. The only subject that bore our constant attack was Chinese medicine. And by hating Chinese medicine so thoroughly, we came to dislike everything that had any con-nection with Chinese culture. Our general opinion was that we should rid our country of the influences of the Chinese altogether. Whenever we met a young student of Chinese literature, we simply felt sorry for him. Particularly were the students of Chinese medicine the butt of our ridicule.[6]

While medicine was the primary focus of those in Dutch Studies, some knowl-edge of Western astronomy, geography, botany, physics, chemistry, and art also

---

[6]E. Kiyooka, trans., *The Autobiography of Fukuzawa Yukichi* (New York: Columbia University Press, 1966), p. 91.

A Tokugawa Skeptic

Confucian teachings, while hardly scientific, placed a premium on rational argument. Some scholars used this rationalism to attack Buddhism. Others directed their attack against superstitions and explanations of natural phenomena which they found wanting. The following passages by Miura Baien (1723–1789), the son of a Kyushu doctor, exemplify such a rationalism.

Does modern science answer the kind of question that Baien is raising? Are some superstitions in modern societies still vulnerable to his critique?

Why do a pair of dark things on the forehead see; why do a pair of holes in the head hear? Why don't eyes hear, why don't ears see? When most people come to these points, they just leave them alone, but I simply can't leave them alone ... They refer the question to past authority, and when they find a book that deals with it, they accept whatever answer it gives. I can't convince myself entirely in that way. When they discuss the natural world, they do so in a wild, hit-or-miss manner; when they talk of life and death, they do so in an absurd or obscure manner. Though their evidence may be flimsy and their arguments preposterous, this does not disturb people at all.

[It is] a human peculiarity is to view everything as human. Take, for example, children's picture books, *The Betrothal of Rats* or *Monsters and Goblins*. Rats are never kept as rats in their true shape; instead all of them are turned into human forms. The bridegroom appears in the book in ceremonial robes with a pair of swords, while the bride is shown with a flowing gown on and snowy cap of cotton, and is carried in a palanquin with an escort of footmen and young guards. In the book of *Monsters and Goblins*, no cases are found of an umbrella turning into a tea-mortar, or of a broom changing into a bucket. But all monsters and goblins are given eyes and noses and hands and feet, so as to look like members of the human family. . . . It is such an imagination as this that populates heaven with a supreme God, and earth with gods of wind and thunder. Monstrous in form, they all move by foot, and do their work by hand. Wind is put in bags, thunder is beaten out on drums. If they are real bags, how were they made? And there must be skin to make a drum. If such imaginings are carried further, the sun will be unable to go on revolving unless it gets feet, and nature will be helpless in her work unless she has hands.

R. Tsunoda, W. T. de Bary, and D. Keene, eds., *Sources of the Japanese Tradition* (New York: Columbia University Press, © 1960), pp. 490, 493–494. Reprinted with permission of the publisher.

entered Japan. Works on science occasionally influenced other thinkers as well. Yamagata Bantō (1748–1821) was a rich and scholarly Osaka merchant who devised a rationalistic philosophy based on a synthesis of Neo-Confucianism and Western science. After studying a work on astronomy, he wrote in 1820 that conditions on other planets "vary only according to their size and their proximity to the sun." He also speculated that "grass and trees will appear, insects will develop; if there are insects, fish, shellfish, animals and birds will not be absent, and finally there will be people too." Bantō qualified his argument with the naturalistic supposition that Mercury and Venus would probably lack human life, "since these two planets are near to the sun and too hot." He contrasted his rational arguments regarding evolution with the "slap-dash" arguments of Buddhists and Shintoists.[7]

From the late 18th century, as Western ships were sighted more frequently in Japanese waters, Japanese began to be aware of the West, and especially Russia, as a threat to Japan. In 1791 a concerned scholar wrote *A Discussion of the Military Problems of a Maritime Nation*, advocating a strong navy and coastal defenses. During the early 19th century, such concerns mounted. A sudden expansion of Dutch Studies occurred after Commodore Matthew Perry's visits to Japan in 1853 and 1854. During the 1860s Dutch Studies became Western Studies, as English, French, German, and Russian were added to the languages studied at the bakufu Institute for the Investigation of Barbarian Books. In sum, Dutch Studies was never a major influence on Tokugawa thought. It cannot begin to compare with Neo-Confucianism. But it laid a foundation on which the Japanese built quickly when the need arose.

LATE TRADITIONAL JAPAN IN HISTORICAL PERSPECTIVE

Historians usually refer to the Tokugawa era as "early modern" since it lies between the "medieval" and the "modern." For many, this is a label of convenience with no serious import. But occasionally the term is employed to suggest that somehow during those centuries Japan prepared for what came next. Such a use of "early modern" misleads in three important respects: first, it seems to locate those centuries of Japanese experience on the continuum of European history. Tokugawa Japan does not fit there, for though points of similarity can be found, the differences were immense. Second, it suggests, following the parallel to early modern Europe, that Japan was in the process of an internal moderization and would have gone on to modernity without further contacts with the West. While a complicated issue, such a proposition is extremely doubtful. Third, it suggests too easy a transition to modernity, a view that belittles the tremendous exertions required of Japanese in the era that followed.

Should the Tokugawa, instead, be called a "late traditional" society? A case can be made for this label. Both the Tokugawa economy and the society with its warrior ruling

---

[7]M. Jansen, ed., *Changing Japanese Attitudes Toward Modernization* (Princeton, NJ: Princeton University Press, 1965), p. 144.

class had evolved out of Warring States Japan. However reshaped, they were extensions of it. Outside influences were minimal. The culture, to be sure, was powerfully affected by a new wave of Chinese learning and the rise of schools and literacy. But after all, Confucianism and Chinese history had been studied in Japan since the Nara period. Despite a quantitative increase so great that it may be seen as qualitative, these cultural elements too were a part of an ongoing tradition. Certainly, when Japanese today talk of what is "traditional," they focus most often on the Tokugawa era—what they like about it they label "Japanese tradition" and what they dislike they call "feudalism."

The problem with "late traditional" is that it may be read as "late static," and such was not the case, for there were major developments in the 17th century and slow changes thereafter. Looking at the outcome of these changes, we can say that its society was more peaceful and productive and its government more competent and sophisticated than ever before in its history. But we cannot simply say that these changes made it able to respond as it did to the West in the mid-19th century. For what was critical in its response was the rapid overthrow of the Tokugawa government and the total revamping of the old society. Scholars still do not see eye to eye over the mix of Tokugawa assets that were critical for its modern development.

In thinking of historical perspective, we must also remember that Europe underwent a transformation during the Tokugawa centuries. Indeed, much of what seems most important in European history—the late Reformation, the scientific revolution of the 17th century, the formation of nation-states, the rise of democracy, the industrial revolution, and the Enlightenment—happened just during those years. If we view Japan from the perspective of Europe, it appears to have been caught in a tar pit of slow motion. But such was not the case; it was actually the West that had accelerated.

SUGGESTED READINGS

H. BOLITHO, *Treasures Among Men: The Fudai Daimyo in Tokugawa Japan* (1974). A study in depth.

C. R. BOXER, *The Christian Century in Japan, 1549–1650* (1951).

M. CHIKAMATSU, *Major Plays of Chikamatsu*, trans. by D. Keene (1961).

R. P. DORE, *Education in Tokugawa Japan* (1965). A pioneer study.

C. J. DUNN, *Everyday Life in Traditional Japan* (1969). A descriptive account of Tokugawa society.

G. S. ELISON, *Deus Destroyed: The Image of Christianity in Early Modern Japan* (1973). A fascinating study of the persecutions of Christianity during the early Tokugawa era.

J. W. HALL, ed., Vol. 4 of the *The Cambridge History of Japan: Early Modern Japan* (1991). Chapters by leading scholars.

J. W. HALL AND M. JANSEN, eds., *Studies in the Institutional History of Early Modern Japan* (1968). A collection of insightful articles on Tokugawa institutions.

H. S. HIBBETT, *The Floating World in Japanese Fiction* (1959). An eminently readable study of early Tokugawa literature.

M. JANSEN, ed., Vol. 5 of *The Cambridge History of Japan: The Nineteenth Century* (1989). Topical chapters by eminent scholars, treating late Tokugawa as well as early Meiji history.

D. KEENE, trans., *Chūshingura, The Treasury of Loyal Retainers* (1971). The puppet play about the 47 rōnin who took revenge on the enemy of their former lord. A valuable source.

M. MARUYAMA, *Studies in the Intellectual History of Tokugawa Japan*, trans. by M. Hane (1974). A seminal work by one of modern Japan's greatest scholars.

K. W. NAKAI, *Shogunal Politics* (1988). A fine study of Arai Hakuseki's conceptualization of Tokugawa government.

P. NOSCO, ed., *Confucianism and Tokugawa Culture* (1984). A solid collection of essays.

H. OOMS, *Charismatic Bureaucrat: A Political Biography of Matsudaira Sadanobu, 1758–1829* (1975). A look at one of the great Tokugawa reformers.

H. OOMS, *Tokugawa Village Practice: Class, Status, Power, Law* (1996).

I. SAIKAKU, *The Japanese Family Storehouse*, trans. by G. W. Sargent (1959). A lively novel about merchant life in 17th-century Japan.

G. B. SANSOM, *The Western World and Japan* (1950). Dated yet contains interesting cultural materials.

C. D. SHELDON, *The Rise of the Merchant Class in Tokugawa Japan* (1958).

T. C. SMITH, *The Agrarian Origins of Modern Japan* (1959). On the evolution of farming and rural social organization in Tokugawa Japan. Fine book.

R. P. TOBY, *State and Diplomacy in Early Modern Japan: Asia in the Development of the Tokugawa Bakufu* (1984). Even during seclusion there was trade.

C. TOTMAN, *Green Archipelago, Forestry in Preindustrial Japan* (1989). An ecological perspective.

C. TOTMAN, *Tokugawa Ieyasu: Shogun* (1983). This book conveys well an era of constant warfare.

K. YAMAMURA AND S. B. HANLEY, *Economic and Demographic Change in Preindustrial Japan, 1600–1868* (1977). Contains provocative thesis regarding birth control in Edo era.

Women textile workers at a turn-of-the-century silk-weaving mill in Japan. Their product, made from mechanically reeled silk thread, was superior. A company officer, at center, is visiting the shop floor. Behind him is a supervisor, wearing a Meiji-style mustache. Women constituted more than half of Japan's industrial labor force well into the 20th century. They worked a span of years after leaving primary school and before marrying. Their hours were long, their dormitories crowded, and they often contracted tuberculosis. [Keystone Press Agency]

chapter four

Modern Japan, 1853–1945

From the mid-19th century to the early 20th, the West was the expanding, aggressive, imperialistic force in world history. Its factories, powered by steam, produced more goods and better goods more cheaply. Its commerce and warships reached every part of the globe. It believed in free trade and used its military might to impose such trade on others. It was the trigger for change throughout the world. But the response to the Western impact varied immensely depending on the internal array of forces in each country. Many countries, unable to respond adequately, became colonies. Some others were forced to cede territory but managed to keep their independence. Of all non-Western nations, only Japan maintained its independence, industrialized, and itself became an imperial power.

OVERTHROW OF THE TOKUGAWA BAKUFU (1853–1868)

Background

A notable feature of Japan's initial response to the West was the rapid collapse of its "ancient regime." At mid-century, the Tokugawa state, older than the United States is today, seemed rocklike in its solidity. No one imagined that it would soon founder. When the regime fell, foreigners resident in Japan saw it as just another proof of Japanese weakness. Yet looking back, we now see the rapid collapse as a positive development that cleared the way for the construction of a new society. In neighboring China, though the foreign impact, in the form of the Opium War, was far more severe, the Ch'ing dynasty recovered and lasted for another 70 years. The recovery kept alive old ideas, values, and vested interests. In Japan the destruction of the Tokugawa state led directly to the destruction of such interests and opened the way for sweeping reforms.

One structural factor contributing to the rapid collapse was the relation of the emperor to the Tokugawa state. As a descendant of the sun goddess, the emperor had a patent of sovereignty—if so recent a concept can be applied to so ancient a notion. Because of this, emperors had always reigned, though other figures usually ruled. During the Tokugawa era, it was the shogun who ruled. Scholars of the Mito domain argued that rule by the Tokugawa was legitimate just because it had been entrusted to them by the sacred emperor. So long as the country was at peace and secure, so long as the emperor and his Kyoto court were tightly controlled by *bakufu* officials, rule by the shogun was accepted. But when Western warships ended seclusion and exposed the country to foreign commerce, and when the "barbarian-conquering" shogun proved unable to deal with the new "barbarians," questions were raised about the legitimacy of shogunal rule. As this occurred, the emperor became detached, as it were, from the *bakufu*-domain system and was used to attack it. Such a development would have been impossible in China, where the emperor both reigned and ruled.

Another structural feature was the role of seclusion in preserving the delicate balance between the small, "hereditary" daimyo who staffed the top offices of the *bakufu* and the large, "outside" daimyo who governed only their own domains. Seclusion enclosed the little world of Tokugawa Japan as the case of a watch encloses its inner workings. The daimyo of large domains resented their lack of a voice in *bakufu* councils—just as low- and middle-ranking samurai of talent and ambition resented the monopoly of domain offices enjoyed by the well-born. But as long as seclusion lasted, such resentments and ambitions had no outlets. When it ended, the large domains and middle and lower samurai took advantages of new opportunities for action, and the system quickly collapsed. Once the case of the watch was removed, the jolt of the foreign intrusion caused the inner workings to fly apart.

Political Process

Commodore Perry came to Japan in 1853, and again in 1854, demanding treaty relations. In the face of the cannon power of the American warships, the *bakufu* had no recourse but to sign a Treaty of Friendship in 1854. The treaty was narrowly defined and provided only for the return of shipwrecked sailors and the supply of coal, food, and water, and these in two areas remote from Edo. Contacts with foreigners were few, and the initial effect on Japan was small. The *bakufu* attended to its affairs as usual and the domains to theirs. Political action consisted mainly of daimyo cliques trying to influence *bakufu* policy; domestic issues remained central.

The break came in 1858, when the *bakufu*, ignoring the imperial court's disapproval, was persuaded to sign a commercial treaty with the United States. The disagreement between the *bakufu* and court fractured the polity at its highest level. Some daimyo, who had long desired a voice in national policy making, said the treaty contravened the hallowed policy of seclusion. A few ambitious young samurai saw it as contrary to the will of the emperor and started a movement to "honor the emperor and expel the barbarian." To silence its critics, the *bakufu* carried out a purge, forcing dissident daimyo into retirement and executing or imprisoning samurai critics. The purge was effective until 1860, when the head of the *bakufu* council was assassinated by extremist samurai. His successors lacked the nerve to continue his tough policies, opening the way for renewed initiatives by large domains between 1861 and 1863.

Chōshū, a domain in southwestern Honshu, was the first to act. It offered to mediate between the court and *bakufu*, ostensibly to heal the rift that had opened over

In this woodblock of 1861, an American sailor tries his hand against a Yokohama sumo wrestler. The official record of Perry's mission to Japan several years earlier tells of a similar experiment with an opposite outcome. Historical truth often depends on who is telling the story. [Courtesy A. Craig]

the commercial treaty. In fact, it was claiming the voice in national politics that it had previously been denied. Its officials traveled between Kyoto and Edo, proposing a policy that favored the *bakufu* while making concessions to the court. The next to emerge was Satsuma, a domain in southern Kyushu, which countered with a policy that made greater concessions to the court and ousted Chōshū from its position as "the friend of the court." The government of Chōshū then adopted the pro-emperor policy of its extremist faction and, in turn, ousted Satsuma. Beaten in the contest of diplomatic negotiations, Satsuma, together with another domain, seized the court in 1863 in a military coup and forced the Chōshū representatives to return disgruntled to their domain.

Five points may be noted about the politics of these years:

1. They took place on a court–*bakufu*, or Kyoto–Edo, axis. Though the court had neither troops nor men of ability, the pro-emperor movement had made it a factor in politics.
2. Even after 250 years of *bakufu* rule, several domains were still viable, autonomous units that could act when the opportunity arose.
3. The two domains that acted first, and most of the others that followed, were big. Chōshū had 10,000 samurai families and substantial financial resources. Satsuma had even more samurai and greater resources.
4. Both Satsuma and Chōshū had fought against Tokugawa armies in 1600 and remembered a more glorious and independent past.
5. By 1863 politics within Chōshū and Satsuma was no longer a monopoly of the daimyo and their high-ranking advisers. Middle- and low-ranking samurai had begun to participate in internal domain affairs in a way that would have been unthinkable ten years earlier.

The 1863 Satsuma coup at the Kyoto court initiated a new phase of politics in which military engagements determined every important turning point. Events were complicated, for besides the court and *bakufu*, there were more than 260 domains. Japan was like a circus with too many rings and sideshows. But most domains were too small to carry weight in national politics. Even "hereditary daimyo" were influential mainly as *bakufu* officials. Of the larger domains, some were insolvent and others too closely associated with the *bakufu* to act independently. As long as Satsuma and Chōshū remained enemies, these several forces stalemated and the *bakufu* continued as hegemon. But once the two domains decided to join forces in 1866, they overthrew the *bakufu* in less than two years.

One source of *bakufu* weakness was a movement by daimyo of a few larger domains for a union of "court and camp." They argued that the *bakufu*, the court, and the larger daimyo should form a ruling national council. Their arguments fell on deaf ears, for the *bakufu* was unwilling to share power. Rebuffed, these daimyo, traditional Tokugawa allies, stood to one side when Chōshū and Satsuma began their campaign to overthrow the *bakufu*.

A second source of *bakufu* weakness was military. The 1858 commercial treaty had provided for the establishment of treaty ports and the residence in them of Western merchants. Samurai extremists, in line with their slogan to "honor the emperor and expel the barbarians," assassinated foreigners as well as *bakufu* officials. Satsuma samurai murdered an English merchant, and Chōshū forts along the Shimonoseki Straits fired on Western ships. But when Western gunboats bombarded the two domains in retaliation, the domains set aside their xenophobic slogan and began buying rifles and gunboats. These purchases upset the balance of military power within Japan. Chōshū formed new rifle companies commanded by lower samurai. Such units—armed with Spencers and Minies, mostly surplus left over from the U.S. Civil War—soundly defeated a numerically superior but traditionally armed *bakufu* army in 1866. The commander of one of these companies was Itō Hirobumi (1841–1909)—a young, low-ranking samurai who would become Japan's first prime minister in 1885.

The court proclaimed the restoration of imperial rule on January 3, 1868. The proclamation was given teeth by an accompanying order stripping the *bakufu* of all its lands. The actual decision was made by representatives of Satsuma, Chōshū, and a few allied domains. Infuriated, the *bakufu* immediately sent troops from the Osaka castle to retake Kyoto but, despite their numerical superiority, they were defeated by Satsuma and Chōshū forces. The shogun and his entourage fled to Edo. Opinion within Japan quickly shifted in favor of the new court government. In May, Edo surrendered to the pro-emperor domains. Within months Edo Castle became the imperial palace and Edo was renamed Tokyo, the "eastern capital." Some domains in northeastern Japan resisted the new government, but they were crushed by the fall of 1868, and in the spring of the following year, the last *bakufu* holdouts surrendered in Hokkaido.

BUILDING THE MEIJI STATE (1868–1890)

Most attempts by non-Western nations to build modern states occurred during the 20th century; in the 19th century even the idea of a "developing nation" did not exist. Yet Japan after the 1868 Meiji Restoration was just such a nation. (The years from 1868 to 1912 are called the "Meiji period," after the emperor's name.) The new government was committed to progress, by which it meant achieving wealth and power of the kind possessed by Western nations. But it had no blueprint for progress, apart from the example of the Western nations, and so it advanced by trial and error, making difficult decisions at every turn. The decisions it took demanded that the Japanese people sacrifice for the sake of the future.

In retrospect, it is clear that Japan had important assets that contributed to the attainment of these goals: a market economy, a fair level of literacy, a stable local society, and a sense of national identity. But it also had liabilities that loomed large in the eyes of the Meiji leaders. The new government directly controlled only the former *bakufu* lands and received income only from those lands. Two thirds of Japan was still occupied by daimyo domains, which paid no taxes to the new government and obeyed its directives only because the government was backed by the Satsuma–Chōshū armies. The country as a whole was poor, and the pools of merchant capital were inadequate to fund modern industries. Literacy was considerably higher than in Russia or Italy, but still, more than half of Japan's

A Japanese View of the Inventiveness of the West

Serious Japanese thinkers reacted to their country's weakness with proposals to adopt Western science and industry. But the "Civilization and Enlightenment Movement" of the 1870s had its lighter side as well. In 1871 the novelist Kanagaki Robun wrote a satire about a man with an umbrella, a watch, and eau de cologne on his hair, who was eating and drinking in a new beef restaurant. Before the Restoration, Buddhism had banned beef eating as a defilement. The comic hero, however, wonders, "Why we in Japan haven't eaten such a clean thing before." He then goes on to rhapsodize about Western inventions.

What do pickled onions have to do with the marvels of Western technology?

In the West they're free of superstitions. There it's the custom to do everything scientifically, and that's why they've invented amazing things like the steamship and the steam engine. Did you know that they engrave the plates for printing newspapers with telegraphic needles? And that they bring down wind from the sky with balloons? Aren't they wonderful inventions! Of course, there are good reasons behind these inventions. If you look at a map of the world you'll see some countries marked "tropical," which means that's where the sun shines closest. The people in those countries are all burnt black by the sun. The king of that part of the world tried all kinds of schemes before he hit on what is called a balloon. That's a big round bag they fill with air high up in the sky. They bring the bag down and open it, causing the cooling air inside the bag to spread out all over the country. That's a great invention. On the other hand, in Russia, which is a cold country where the snow falls even in summer and the ice is so thick that people can't move, they invented the steam engine. You've got to admire them for it. I understand that they modeled the steam engine after the flaming chariot of hell, but anyway, what they do is to load a crowd of people on a wagon and light a fire in a pipe underneath. They keep feeding the fire inside the pipe with coal, so that the people riding on top can travel a great distance completely oblivious to the cold. Those people in the West can think up inventions like that, one after the other. . . . You say you must be going? Well, good-bye. Waitress! Another small bottle of sake. And some pickled onions to go with it!

From Modern Japanese Literature, D. Keene, ed. and trans. pp. 32–33. Copyright © 1956 Grove Press. Reprinted by permission of Grove/Atlantic, Inc.

population could not read or write. Samurai could, but few of them were forward-looking. Their education in Chinese texts did not meet the needs of a developing state. Technology was appreciated but little understood, despite the impetus of Dutch Studies.

Centralization of Power

At its inception the new Meiji government was no more than a handful of samurai leaders from Chōshū, Satsuma, and their allied domains. They were young—in their 30s or 40s. They were middle or lower in rank, not from the thin upper stratum that had ruled prior to 1861. They had risen to power as domain policy makers and as commanders of new domain armies. Like Washington or Lincoln in the United States, even today their names have a mythic resonance in Japan. The top leaders were Kido Takayoshi of Chōshū, Ōkubo Toshimichi and Saigō Takamori of Satsuma, and Ōkuma Shigenobu of Saga.

The leaders controlled the young emperor through two nobles sympathetic to their rule. They controlled the domain armies of Chōshū and Satsuma through personal ties to their commanders, many of whom later entered the new central government. The new leaders have been described, half-humorously, as 12 bureaucrats in search of a bureaucracy. Such a description does not do justice to the vision with which they defined the goals of the new government. But most important, perhaps, was that they had no stake in the old Tokugawa system. Backed by the domain armies of Chōshū and Satsuma, they moved ruthlessly against vested interests.

Their first target was the daimyo domains. They began by whittling down their autonomy and then, in 1871, replaced them with prefectures administered directly by the central government. This was a slow and delicate process, since many in the new domain armies were of two minds about the young samurai leaders who had abandoned their domains to form the new government. To ensure a complete break with the past, each new prefectural governor was chosen from samurai of other regions. The first governor of the Chōshū area, for example, was a samurai from a former Tokugawa domain. Once the domains were abolished, their tax revenues flowed directly to Tokyo.

Having centralized political authority in 1871, half of the most important Meiji leaders went abroad for a year and a half, purportedly to revise the unequal treaties but also to study the nations they hoped to emulate. They traveled to the United States and Europe, visiting parliaments, schools, and factories. On returning to Japan in 1872, they discovered that the stay-at-home officials were planning war with Korea. They quickly quashed the plan, insisting that the highest priority be given to domestic development.

A second goal of the Meiji leaders was to stabilize government revenues. As before, most of the land tax was collected in kind, and revenues fluctuated with the price of rice. The government converted the grain tax to a money tax, shifting the burden of fluctuations onto the shoulders of the nation's farmers. As compensation, they gave farmers and some landlords titles of ownership to their lands. But a third of tax revenues still went to pay for samurai stipends, so in 1873, the government raised a conscript army and soon after abolished the samurai class. The samurai were paid off in government bonds, but as the bonds fell during the inflation of the 1870s, most former samurai became impoverished. What had begun as a reform of government finance ended as a social revolution.

Some samurai rebelled. Those in the domains that had carried out the Restoration were particularly indignant at their treatment. The last and greatest uprising was by Satsuma samurai in 1877. It was led by a reluctant Saigō Takamori (1827–1877), who had broken with the government over the issue of Korea. With the suppression of the uprising in 1878, the Meiji government became militarily secure.

New Ideas

Throughout the Tokugawa era, educated Japanese had seen themselves as Confucian and civilized; the rest of the world was barbarian, China and Korea excepted. Perry and the other Westerners who came to Japan were labeled as such. But the military technology of the West soon called this view into question: How could "barbarians" build steamships that crossed the oceans of the world? As an explanation, in the late 1860s, Fukuzawa Yukichi (1835–1901), a student of Western studies and a *bakufu* translator, introduced into Japan the prevalent Western view of history in which the West, with its technology, science, and humane laws was seen as "civilized and enlightened," China, Japan, Turkey, and several other countries were seen as "half-civilized," and the rest of the world was seen as barbarian. This theory of the stages of history stood the traditional view on its head.

As a corollary, Fukuzawa argued that the technology that made the West so strong was not detachable but grew out of Western political, economic, legal, and educational systems. He cited the case of the Englishman James Watt, who in part had been moved to invent the steam engine because inventions were protected by patents and inventors were rewarded with profits and honors. The benefits of technology, Fukuzawa further contended, could only be acquired by a nation with an independent citizenry and a legal system for protecting human rights.

Fukuzawa's books were widely read during the last years or two before the Restoration and became best sellers during the early Meiji. His writings sparked the "Civilization and Enlightenment movement" of the 1870s. Leaders of the movement, who, like Fukuzawa, had begun as students of Dutch Studies, delivered "enlightened" opinions on subjects as diverse as constitutional government, philosophy, education, religion, natural rights, marriage, wives and concubines, and prostitution. Their ideas spread just at the time the government was building new Western-style institutions and those seeking a voice in politics were looking for an ideology to justify an opposition movement.

The Cultural Revolution of Meiji Japan: Westerners' Views

While the political parties prepared for constitutional government and the government built dikes to contain the parties, Japan's society and culture were being transformed.

ON JAPANESE STUDENTS IN 1868

What a sight for a schoolmaster! . . . They are all dressed in the native costume of loose coats, with long and bag-like sleeves; kilts, like petticoats, open at the upper side; with shaven midscalps, and topknots like gun-hammers. Men and boys carry slates and copy books in their hands, and common cheap glass ink bottles slung by pieces of twine to their girdles. Hands and faces are smeared with the black fluid; but, strangest of all, each has two of the murderous-looking swords, one long and the other short, stuck in his belt. Symbols of the soldier rather than the scholar are these; but the samurai are both.

ON JAPAN DURING THE 1870s

To understand the situation you have to realize that less than ten years ago the Japanese were living under conditions like those of our chivalric age and the feudal system of the Middle Ages, with its monasteries, guilds, Church universal, and so on; but that betwixt night and morning, one might almost say, and with one great leap, Japan is trying to traverse the stages of five centuries of European development, and to assimilate in the twinkling of an eye all the latest achievements of western civiliza-

tion. The country is thus undergoing an immense cultural revolution—for the term "evolution" is inapplicable to a change so rapid and so fundamental. I feel myself lucky to be an eyewitness of so interesting an experiment.

LOOKING BACK FROM THE 1890s

If one considers the comparative precocity of the Japanese youth, as well as the wild and lawless traditions which students of twenty years ago had inherited from their predecessors, and adds thereto the further consideration that twenty years ago parental authority was at its lowest in Japan, for the reason that the go-ahead sons were conscious of knowing a great deal more than their old-fashioned, old world parents, . . . it will not be wondered at that in those early days strikes sometimes took place which bore a striking testimony to the power of organization which is innate in the Japanese. . . . But I am talking of events which took place many years ago. Things are very much changed now. . . . The go-ahead student of twenty years ago is the go-ahead parent of today, and has succeeded in reestablishing over his children that parental authority which for the time slipped from the grasp of his old world father.

W. E. Griffis, *The Mikado's Empire* (New York: Harper and Brothers, 1896), p. 370; E. Baelz, *Awakening Japan: The Diary of a German Doctor* (New York: Viking Press, 1932), p. 16; A. Lloyd, *Everyday Japan* (New York: Cassell and Co., 1909), pp. 272–273.

On Wives and Concubines

During the 1870s and 1880s leading Japanese thinkers introduced a wide range of Western ideas into their country. Among them were freedom and equality as rights inherent in human nature. Debating the questions of equality in marriage and the rights of wives, intellectuals voiced a radical criticism of concubinage and prostitution. As a consequence of these debates, laws were passed during the eighties and nineties that strengthened the legal status of wives. Mori Arinori (1847–1889), a leading thinker who had studied in the United States and England, wrote the following passage in 1874. He later became a diplomat and, between 1885 and 1889, the minister of education.

Can you think of a comparable instance in American or European history when new ideas led to dramatic social change? How long did the changes last and how deeply rooted did they become?

The relation between man and wife is the fundamental of human morals. The moral path will be achieved by establishing this fundamental, and the country will only be firmly based if the moral path is realized. When people marry, rights and obligations emerge between them so that neither can take advantage of the other.

There have hitherto been a variety of marriage practices [in our country]. . . . Sometimes there may be one or even several concubines in addition to the wife, and sometimes a concubine may become the wife. Sometimes the wife and the con-cubines live in the same establishment. Sometimes they are separated, and the concubine is the favored one while the wife is neglected. . . .

Taking a concubine is by arbitrary decision of the man and with acquiescence of the concubine's family. The arrangement, known as *ukedashi*, is made by paying money to the family of the concubine. This means, in other words, that concubines are bought with money. Since concubines are generally *geisha* and prostitutes patronized by rich men and nobles, many descendants in the rich and noble houses are the children of bought women. Even though the wife is superior to the concubine in households where they live together, there is commonly jealousy and hatred between them because the husband generally favors the concubine. Therefore, there are numerous instances when, the wife and the concubines being scattered in separate establishments, the husband repairs to the abode of the one with whom he is infatuated and wilfully resorts to scandalous conduct. . . .

Thus, I have here explained that our country has not yet established the fundamental of human morality, and I hope later to discuss how this situation injures our customs and obstructs enlightenment.

From *Journal of the Japanese Enlightenment* by Meiroku Zasshi, translated and with introduction by William Reynolds Braisted, assisted by Adachi Yasushi and Kikuchi Yūji (Cambridge, MA: Harvard University Press, 1976), pp. 104–105. © 1976 by the President and Fellows of Harvard College. Reprinted by permission of Harvard University Press.

Political Parties

The swift suppression of the Satsuma uprising proved the futility of rebellion. From the mid-1870s disgruntled samurai began to form political parties and campaign for popular rights, elections, and a constitution. They drew heavily on liberal Western models. They argued that national assemblies were the means by which advanced societies tapped the energies of their peoples. The formation of such an assembly in Japan, they maintained, would unite the emperor and the people, thereby curbing the arbitrary rule of the Satsuma–Chōshū clique. Samurai were the mainstay of the early party movement, despite its doctrines proclaiming all classes to be equal.

To placate the rising opposition, in 1878 the government established prefectural assemblies. Many people's rights activists were elected to these bodies, and, as elections were held, what had been in fact unofficial pressure groups became true political parties. Farmers joined, hoping to have their taxes cut; the poor joined, too, hoping to improve their condition. The parties were given another boost when, following a scandal and political crisis in 1881, the government promised a constitution and a national assembly within ten years. During the 1880s, the parties had ups and downs. When poorer farmers rebelled, the parties temporarily dissolved to dissociate themselves from the uprisings. But as the date for national elections approached, they reorganized and regained strength, and the ties between party notables and local men of influence grew closer.

The Meiji Constitution

The government viewed the party movement with distaste but was unsure how to combat it. The promise of a constitution had been one tactic. In 1882 Itō Hirobumi (1841–1909), now a powerful government leader, went to Europe to look for a constitution that would serve the needs of the Meiji government. He found principles to his liking in Germany and brought back a German jurist to help adapt the conservative Prussian Constitution of 1850 to Japanese uses. As promulgated in 1889, the Meiji Constitution was notable for the extensive powers it granted to the emperor and for the severely limited powers it granted to the lower house in the Diet (the English term for Japan's bicameral national assembly).

According to the constitution, the emperor was sovereign. He was "sacred and inviolable," and in Itō's commentaries, the sacredness was defined in Shinto terms. As in Prussia, the emperor was given direct command of the armed forces. A German-type general staff system had already been set up in 1878 by Yamagata Aritomo (1838–1922), who, like Itō, had begun as a military commander in Chōshū. The emperor had the right to name the prime minister and to appoint the Cabinet. He could dissolve the lower house of the Diet and issue imperial ordinances when the

Diet was not in session. The Imperial Household Ministry, which was outside the Cabinet, administered the great wealth given to the imperial family during the 1880s—so that the emperor would never have to ask Diet politicians for funds. It was intended and understood that the Meiji leaders would act in the name of the emperor in all of these matters. The constitution itself was presented as a gift from the emperor to his subjects.

The lower house of the Diet was given the authority only to approve budgets and pass laws, and both of these powers were hedged. The constitution stipulated that the previous year's budget would remain in effect if a new budget was not approved. The appointive House of Peers, the upper house of the Diet, had to approve any bill for it to become law. Furthermore, to ensure that the parties them-selves would represent the stable and responsible elements of Japanese society, the vote was given only to adult males paying 15 yen or more in taxes. In 1890 this came to about five percent of the adult male population. In short, Itō had not intended to create a parliamentary system with full deliberative powers. What he devised was a constitutional system that contained as one of its parts a parliament.

The government also created institutions to limit the future influence of the political parties. In 1884 it created a new nobility with which to stock the House of Peers. The nobility, honorable and conservative, was composed of ex-nobles and the Meiji leaders themselves. Itō, who was by birth a lowly foot soldier, began in the new nobility as a count and ended as a prince. In 1885 he established a cabinet system and became the first prime minister. He was followed by Kuroda Kiyotaka (1840–1900) of Satsuma and then by Yamagata Aritomo. In 1887 Itō established a Privy Council, with himself as its head, to approve the constitution he had written. In 1888 new laws and civil service examinations were instituted to insulate the imperial bureaucracy from the tawdry concerns of party politics. By then, the bureaucracy, which had begun as a loose collection of men of ability and their protégés, had become highly systematized. Detailed administrative laws defined officials' functions and governed their behavior. They were well paid: middle-ranking officials could afford to visit geisha. In 1890 there were 24,000 officials; in 1908 there were 72,000.

GROWTH OF A MODERN ECONOMY

The late Tokugawa economy was backward, not markedly different from the economies of other East Asian countries. Almost 80 percent of the population lived in the countryside at a near subsistence level. Paddy-field techniques were advanced but labor-intensive. Taxes were high, as much as 30 to 35 percent of the product, and two thirds of the land tax was paid in kind. Money had only partially penetrated the rural economy. Japan lacked machine-based factory production, steam power, and large accumulations of capital.

Early Meiji reforms unshackled the late Tokugawa economy. Occupations were freed, which meant that farmers could trade and samurai could farm. Barriers on roads were abolished, as were the monopolistic guilds that had restricted access to central markets. The abolition of domains threw open regional economies that had been partially self-enclosed. The majority of large merchant houses were too closely tied to daimyo finances and went bankrupt, but there rose a groundswell of new commercial ventures and of traditional agriculturally based industries.

Silk was the wonder crop. The government introduced mechanical reeling, enabling Japan to win markets previously held by the hand-reeled silk of China. About two thirds of Japanese silk production was exported, and not until the 1930s did cotton textiles become a more important export. Silk production rose from 2.3 million pounds in the post-Restoration era to 16 million at the turn of the century, to 93 million on the eve of the Great Depression in 1929.

A shift toward freer markets also occurred on the land. Forward-looking landlords took advantage of fixed tax rates; they increased production using fertilizers and farm machinery and emerged as a new and prosperous rural class. Overall, rice production rose from 149 million bushels a year during 1880–1884 to 316 million during 1935–1937. More food, combined with a lower death rate—the result of better hygiene—led to population growth, from 30 million in 1868, to 45 million in 1900, to 73 million in 1940. Because the number engaged in farming remained constant, the extra hands became available for factory and other urban jobs. But fixed tax rates often hurt small farmers. In the deflation of the 1880s, when the prices of agricultural products fell, many were forced to sell their small plots. Tenancy rose from an estimated 25 percent in 1868 to 44 percent at the turn of the century. Tenants, who paid rents in kind, did not share in the new prosperity.

First Phase: Model Industries

The development of modern industry was the government's highest priority. It developed in four phases. The first, which lasted until 1881, was the era of model industries. The government expanded the arsenals and the shipyards it had inherited from the Tokugawa. It also built telegraph lines; made a start on railroads; developed coal and copper mines; and established factories for cotton-spinning, cement, glass, tools, and other products. Every new industry begun during the 1870s was the work of the government, many initiated by the Ministry of Industry, set up in 1870 under Itō. The quantitative output of these early industries was insignificant, however. Essentially they were pilot-plant operations that doubled as "schools" for technologists and labor.

Just as important to economic development were other new institutions such as banks, post offices, ports, roads, commercial laws, a public system of primary and secondary schools, and a government university. All were patterned on European and American models, although the pattern was often altered to fit Japan's needs; Tokyo Imperial University, for example, had a faculty of agriculture earlier than any university in Europe.

Second Phase: 1880s–1890s

More substantial growth in the modern sector took place during the 1880s and 1890s. It was marked by the appearance of what would later become the great industrial combines known as *zaibatsu*. Accumulating capital was the greatest problem for would-be entrepreneurs. Iwasaki Yatarō (1834–1885) used political connections. After the Restoration, he bought up the ships he formerly had managed as a Tosa domain samurai official. He next acquired government ships that had been used to transport troops during an 1874 military expedition to Taiwan and the 1877 Satsuma Rebellion. From these beginnings, he built a shipping line to compete with foreign companies, started a bank, and invested in the enterprises that later became the Mitsubishi combine.

Shibusawa Eiichi (1840–1931) was a maverick entrepreneur. Born into a prosperous peasant family that made indigo dye, he helped his father buy the raw material and sell the finished dye, briefly organized a local anti-*bakufu* group, then switched sides and became a retainer of the last shogun. He spent two years in France, and after the 1868 Restoration, entered the Finance Ministry. In 1873 he made the so-called heavenly descent from government to private business. Founding the First Bank, he showed a talent for beginning new industries with other people's money. His initial success was the Osaka Cotton Spinning Mill, established as Japan's first joint stock company in 1882. The investors profited hugely, and money poured in to found new mills; in 1896 the production of yarn had reached 17 million pounds, and in 1913 more than ten times that amount. After the turn of the century, cotton cloth replaced yarn as the focus of modern growth in Japan: production rose more than 100-fold, from 22 million square yards in 1900 to 2.7 billion in 1936.

Another area of growth was railroads. Before railroads, the bulk of Japan's commerce had been carried by coastal shipping. It cost as much during the early Meiji period to transport goods 50 miles overland as it did to ship them to Europe. Railroads gave Japan an internal circulatory system, opening up hitherto isolated regions. In 1872 Japan had 18 miles of track; in 1894, 2100 miles; and in 1934, 14,500 miles.

Cotton textiles and railroads were followed during the 1890s by cement, bricks, matches, glass, beer, chemicals, and other private industries. One can only admire the foresight and daring of entrepreneurs like Iwasaki and Shibusawa who pioneered in these industries. At the same time, one should not forget the role of government in creating a favorable climate for growth. State and society were stable, the yen was sound, capital was safe, and taxes on industry were extremely low.

Natsume Sōseki on the Costs of Rapid Modernization

Natsume Sōseki (1867–1916) was one of the earliest of a series of great novelists to create a new literature in Japan after the turn of the century. Sōseki could often be humorous. One of his early works, *I Am a Cat*, looked at a Tokyo household from a feline perspective. He advocated ethical individualism as superior to state morality. He also wrote of human isolation in a changing society and of the dark side of human nature.

What were the costs of Japan's rapid modernization? Was the uneasiness experienced by only a few advanced thinkers, or did it cut across the society? Was it different from alienation in the modern West?

My Individualism

Let us set aside the question of the bragging about the new teachings acquired from the West, which are only superficially mastered. Let us suppose that in forty or fifty years after the Restoration, by the power of education, by really applying ourselves to study, we can move from teaching A to teaching B and even advance to C— without the slightest vulgar fame-seeking,

without the slightest sense of vainglory. Let us further suppose that we pass, in a natural orderly fashion, from stage to stage and that we ultimately attain the extreme of differentiation in our internally developed enlightenment that the West attained after more than a hundred years. If, then, by our physical and mental exertions, and by ignoring the difficulties and suffering involved in our precipitous advance, we end by passing through, in merely one-half the time it took the more prosperous Westerners to reach their stage of specialization, to our stage of internally developed enlightenment, the consequences will be serious indeed. At the same time we will be able to boast of this fantastic acquisition of knowledge, the inevitable result will be a nervous collapse from which we will not be able to recover.

Passers-by

This is what your brother said. He suffers because nothing he does appears to him as either an end or a means. He is perpetually uneasy and cannot relax. He cannot sleep and so gets out of bed. But when he is awake, he cannot stay still, so he begins to

Third Phase: 1905–1929

The economy continued to expand after the Russo-Japanese War in 1904–1905, and spurted ahead during World War I. Light industries and textiles remained central, but iron and steel, shipping, coal mining, electrical power, and chemicals also grew. An economic slump followed the war, and the economy grew slowly during the 1920s. One factor was renewed competition from a Europe at peace. Another was the great earthquake that destroyed Tokyo in 1923. Tokyo was rebuilt with loans from abroad,

walk. As he walks, he finds that he has to begin running. Once he has begun running, he cannot stop. To have to keep on running is bad enough, but he feels compelled to increase his speed with every step he takes. When he imagines what the end of all this will be, he is so frightened that he breaks out in a cold sweat. And the fear becomes unbearable.

I was surprised when I heard your brother's explanation. I myself have never experienced uneasiness of this kind. And so, though I could comprehend what he was saying, I could feel no sympathy for him. I was like a man who tries to imagine what it is like to have a splitting headache though he has never had one. I tried to think for a while. And my wandering mind hit upon this thing called "man's fate"; it was a rather vague concept in my mind, but I was happy to have found something consoling to say to your brother.

"This uneasiness of yours is no more than the uneasiness that all men experience. All you have to do is to realize that there is no need for you alone to worry so much about it. What I mean to say is that it is our fate to wander blindly through life."

Not only were my words vague in meaning but they lacked sincerity. Your brother gave me one shrewd, contemptuous glance; that was all my remarks deserved. He then said:

"You know, our uneasiness comes from this thing called scientific progress. Science does not know where to stop and does not permit us to stop either. From walking to rickshaws, from rickshaws to horsedrawn cabs, from cabs to trains, from trains to automobiles, from automobiles to airships, from airships to airplanes—when will we ever be allowed to stop and rest? Where will it finally take us? It is really frightening."

"Yes, it is frightening," I said.

Your brother smiled.

"You say so, but you don't really mean it. You aren't really frightened. This fear that you say you feel, it is only of the theoretical kind. My fear is different from yours. I feel in my heart. It is an alive, pulsating kind of fear."

First selection from *Japanese Thought in the Meiji Era* by M. Kosaka. Copyright © 1958 Pan-Pacific Press, pp. 447–448; Second selection from "An Introduction to Sōseki," by E. McClellan. *Harvard Journal of Asiatic Studies*, 22 (December 1959), pp. 205–207.

but they led to inflation. Agricultural productivity also leveled off during the 1920s; it became cheaper to import foodstuffs from the newly acquired colonies of Taiwan and Korea than to invest in new agricultural technology at home.

By the 1920s Japanese society, especially urban society, was becoming modern. The Japanese ate better, were healthier, and lived longer. Personal savings rose with the standard of living. Urban workers opened postal saving accounts, drank beer, went to movies, and read newspapers and magazines. In 1890 31 percent of girls and 64 percent of boys went to primary schools; in 1905 the figures were 90 and 96 percent;

by 1925 primary school education was mandatory for all. Japan had done what no other non-Western nation had even attempted: it had achieved universal literacy. During the 1920s, 1930s, and war years, increasing numbers of primary school graduates went on to middle and higher schools or entered new technical colleges. Even so, an enormous cultural and social gap remained between the majority who had only a primary or secondary school education and the three percent who attended university. This gap would prove to be a basic weakness in the political democracy of the twenties.

Despite the overall improvements, the human costs of growth were often high. Because of the predominant role of textiles in the early phase of modern economic growth, well into the 20th century, more than half of the industrial labor force was women. They went to the mills after leaving primary school and returned to their villages before marrying. "Neither silk-reeling maids nor slops are kept for long," went the words of one song. Their working hours were long, their dormitories crowded, and their movements restricted. "Like the money in my employment contract, I remain sealed away," was another verse. Many contracted tuberculosis, the "white plague" of late 19th- and early 20th-century Japan, and were sent back to their villages to die. The following verse captures the general public attitude toward women factory workers:

> If a woman working in an office is a willow,
> A poetess is a violet,
> And a female teacher is an orchid,
> Then a factory woman is a vegetable gourd.[1]

Fourth Phase: Depression and Recovery

A Japanese bank crisis in 1927, followed by the worldwide Great Depression in 1929, plunged Japan into unemployment and suffering. The distress was particularly acute in the rice-producing northeast, where there were few by-employments to fall back on. But Japan's recovery was relatively rapid, more so than that of any other industrial nation. Most of Japan had recovered by 1933, and even the northeast by 1935.

The recovery was fueled by cheap yen, which led to an export boom, and by military procurements at home. During the 1930s the production of pig iron, raw steel, and chemicals doubled. Japan was able to construct complete electric-power stations and be self-sufficient in machine tools and scientific instruments. Shipbuilding forged

---

[1]E. Patricia Tsurumi, "Whose History Is It Anyway? And Other Questions Historians Should Be Asking," in *Japan Review* (1995) 6:17–38, p. 21. By permission of the International Center for Japanese Studies.

ahead; in 1937 Japan had a merchant fleet of 4.5 million tons, the third largest and certainly the newest in the world. Despite continued growth in cotton cloth during the 1930s, textiles slipped relative to the products of heavy industry. The quality of Japan's manufacturers also rose. The outcry in the West against Japanese exports at this time was not so much because of volume—a modest 3.6 percent of world exports in 1936—but because for the first time Japanese products had become competitive in terms of quality.

THE POLITICS OF IMPERIAL JAPAN (1890–1927)

Parliaments began in the West, where they have functioned better than in the rest of the world. For Japan to establish a parliament during the 19th century was a bold experiment. However limited its powers, it was the first parliament outside the West. When it opened in 1890, most Western observers were skeptical of its chances for success. In retrospect, how are we to view the Japanese experiment in parliamentary government?

Some scholars argue that the Japanese were not ready for parliamentary government and thus the militarism of the 1930s was inevitable. Certainly, from an ideal perspective, Japanese society had weaknesses: a small middle class, weak trade unions, a limited suffrage, few rights for women, a strong emperor-centered nationalism, a military directly responsible only to a figurehead emperor, and so on. Had Japanese society been otherwise, militarism might not have arisen.

Others contend that militarism was not inevitable. Japan's internal weaknesses were not surprising, considering that Japan in 1890 was just two decades removed from a society of daimyo domains and two-sworded samurai. That the new Diet could function at all was a marvel. But the weaknesses neither prevented the Diet from growing in importance nor blocked the transfer of power from the Restoration leaders to political party presidents. The transfer, admittedly, fell short of full parliamentary government, but had it not been derailed by the Great Depression and other external factors, the advance toward a parliamentary state might have continued during the 1930s.

Diet Politics, the First Decade

The Meiji Constitution had been promulgated in 1889. An election was held and the first Diet opened in 1890. At the time the Meiji leaders saw themselves as nation builders. They drew up budgets, improved the military services, refined the banking system, established new universities, further reformed the tax system, prosecuted wars—all of those activities that characterized a dynamic 19th century state.

The leaders, sometimes referred to as *oligarchs*, the few who rule, saw the cabinet as "transcendental," as an institution that served the emperor and nation above the ruck of partisan interests. They viewed the lower house of the new Diet as a safety valve, where the political parties, noisy, irresponsible, and ineffective, could blow off steam and vent opinions without interferring in the serious work of building a new Japan.

But Itō had miscalculated. The authority of the lower house to approve or veto budgets made that body more powerful than he had intended. Consequently, the oligarchs were drawn, willy-nilly, into the partisan political struggles they had hoped to avoid.

The first act of the parties in the new 1890 Diet was to slash the government's budget. Prime Minister Yamagata was furious but had to make concessions to get part of the cut restored. This tactic of applying pressure to reduce the annual budget continued for almost a decade, and rising costs meant that the previous year's budget was never enough. The government tried to intimidate and bribe the parties but failed. It then formed its own party and tried to win elections by enlisting the police and local officials, but this, too, failed. The nongovernmental opposition parties continued to win a majority of seats in the lower house. They had well-organized constituencies in

The first Diet opened in 1890 during the ministry of Yamagata Aritomo. The Emperor Meiji, with sword, sits on the right under a canopy. The empress, with her ladies-in-waiting, can be seen at the upper left. This two-story building, located at the western corner of Hibiya Park, burned down in January 1891. A new Diet building was built by October of the same year. [Bettmann/Hulton]

the prefectures, where assemblies had begun in 1878, and they also had the support of voters, mostly well-to-do landowners, who opposed the heavy land tax.

Unable to coerce or defeat the opposition parties and determined that his constitution not fail, Itō changed his tactics in 1900 and coopted one wing of the opposition. He brought together a group of ex-bureaucrats and the Liberal Party, which had been founded by a Tosa samurai, Itagaki Taisuke (1837–1919) in 1881. He called his new party the Rikken Seiyūkai or Friends of Consitutional Government. For the next 20 years it was the dominant party in the lower house and provided support for successive governments. This arrangement satisfied both sides: The party politicians, hitherto excluded, got cabinet posts and pork barrel legislation with which to reward their supporters. Itō and subsequent prime ministers got the lower house support necessary for the smooth functioning of "constitutional governent." By creating the new party, Itō had made the constitution work, but at the cost of sacrificing transcendental cabinets.

The Golden Years of Meiji

The years before and after the turn of the century represented the culmination of what the government had striven for since 1868. Economic development was underway. The unequal treaties of the pre-Restoration years were revised in two steps: Japan got rid of extraterritoriality in 1899 (by a treaty signed in 1894) and regained control of its tariffs in 1911. But it was only when imperial Japan became imperialist Japan that it was accorded recognition as a world power.

The first step was war with China in 1894–1895 over conflicting interests in Korea. Western observers expected China to win, but the Japanese, using modern naval tactics, sank the Chinese fleet and also won on land. From its victory, Japan secured Taiwan, the Pescadores Islands, the Kwantung Peninsula in southern Manchuria, an indemnity, and a treaty giving it the same privileges in China as those given to the Western powers (see Map 4-1). Russia, however, had its own expansionist plans for East Asia and, obtaining French and German support, forced Japan to give up the Kwantung Peninsula, which included Port Arthur. Three years later, Russia took the peninsula for itself.

The second step was Japan's participation in 1900 in the international force that relieved the siege of the foreign legation quarter in Peking by an antiforeign rebel force known as the Boxers. Western observers commented on the number, courage, and discipline of the Japanese troops.

The third step was the Anglo-Japanese Alliance in 1902. For Britain the alliance ensured Japanese support for its East Asian interests and forestalled the possibility of a Russian-Japanese agreement over spheres of influence in Northeast Asia. For Japan the alliance meant that it could fight Russia without fear that a third party would intervene.

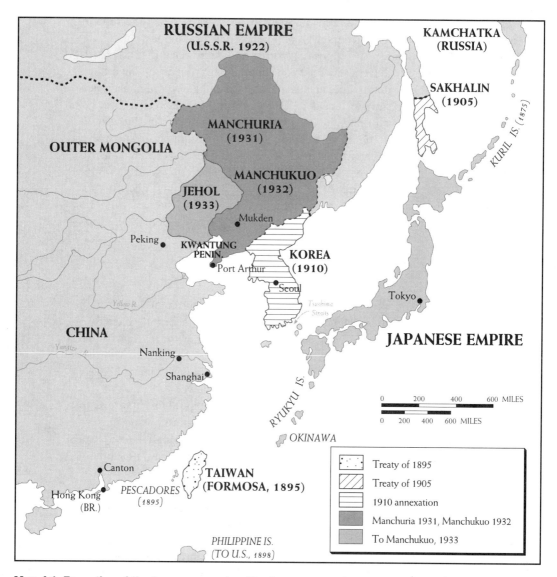

Map 4-1 Formation of the Japanese empire. The Japanese empire grew in three stages: The Sino-Japanese War in 1894–1895, the Russo-Japanese War of 1904–1905, and Japanese conquests in Manchuria and Northern China.

The fourth step was the war with Russia. Early in 1904 Japanese torpedo boats launched a surprise attack on the Russian fleet at Port Arthur. On land, Japanese armies drove the Russians from their railway zones in Manchuria and seized Mukden in March 1905. The Russians sent their Baltic fleet to join the battle, but

Japanese troops take the fort at Port Arthur in 1904 in a major battle of the Russo-Japanese War. Fifteen thousand Japanese were killed in this battle, ten times the losses of the Russians. [Corbis-Bettmann]

it was annihilated by Admiral Tōgō at the Tsushima Straits. After months of war, both countries were worn out and, on the homefront, Russia was plagued by revolution. President Theodore Roosevelt proposed a peace conference at Portsmouth, New Hampshire. The resulting treaty gave Japan the Russian lease in the Kwantung Peninsula, the Russian railway in south Manchuria, the southern half of Sakhalin, and a recognition of Japan's "paramount interest" in Korea, which it annexed in 1910.

It is ironic that Japan, a country still not free of the system of unequal treaties, should have joined the imperialist scramble for colonies. Certainly, the desire for colonies is not to be explained by Japanese tradition, which, Hideyoshi apart, had rarely looked to foreign expansion. Nor, despite some trading advantages that provided profits for a few, is it to be explained by Japan's economy, which was just beginning to build modern industries and had no surplus capital for export. The explanation is simpler: Japan wanted equality with the great powers; military strength and colonies were the best credentials. Enthusiasm for empire was shared alike by party politicians, conservative leaders, and most liberal thinkers.

Rise of the Parties to Power

The founding of the Seiyūkai by Itō in 1900 had ended a decade of confrontation between the Diet and the government. The aging oligarch Itō soon found intolerable the constant bickering of party politicians, who, unlike the bureaucrats, neither obeyed him nor paid him the simple respect he thought his due. In 1903 he relinquished the presidency of the party to the noble Saionji Kinmochi (1849–1940). Saionji also found the post too much to bear and passed it to Hara Takashi (1856–1921) in 1914. With Hara, the office found the man.

Hara was an outsider. Born a generation after the founding fathers of the Meiji state in a politically unimportant northeastern domain, he began his political career as a newspaper reporter. He then entered the Foreign Ministry, eventually becoming minister to Korea, and in turn, a newspaper editor, bank official, company president, and Diet member. Perspicacious, patient, painstaking, and paternalistic, he helped Itō found the Seiyūkai and was regarded as the most able politician in Japan. As the president of the Seiyūkai, his goals for Japan centered on the expansion of national wealth and power—little different from those of Itō or Yamagata. But he felt that they should be achieved by party government, not oligarchic rule, and worked unceasingly to expand the power of his party. The years between 1905 and 1921 were marked by the struggle between these two alternative conceptions of government.

The struggle can be represented as a rising curve of party strength and a descending curve of oligarchic influence. The rising curve had two vectors: a buildup of the Seiyūkai party machine, which enabled it to win elections and maintain itself as the majority (or plurality) party in the Diet, and the strengthening of the Diet vis-à-vis other elites within the government in Tokyo. For the former, Hara obtained campaign funds from industrialists and other moneyed interests, and promoted pork barrel legislation in the Diet. Local constituencies that supported Seiyūkai candidates got new schools, bridges, dams, roads, or even railroad lines. Seiyūkai politicians established ties with local notables who brokered the votes of their communities. Hara served as home minister in three cabinets and was not averse to calling on local police and officials to aid Seiyūkai election campaigns.

In co-opting other governmental elites, the Seiyūkai had mixed success. The party steadily increased its representation in the cabinet. It gained some patronage appointments in the central bureaucracy and the newly formed colonial bureaucracy. These officials were beholden to the party, but most other bureaucrats saw themselves as professionals and resisted party affiliation. In the conservative House of Peers and in the Privy Council, which had the power to ratify treaties, the Seiyūkai fared less well. By and large, they remained independent bodies. The Seiyūkai had no success in penetrating the military services. At best, it exercised some restraints on military budgets in time of peace.

The descending curve of weakening oligarchic control reflected the aging of the "men of Meiji." In 1900 Itō was the last oligarch to become prime minister. From 1901 to 1912, Saionji Kinmochi, Itō's protégé, and Katsura Tarō (1847–1913), a general born in Chōshū and a protégé of Yamagata, took turns in the post. Both had Seiyūkai support. Toward the end, Katsura began to resent the need to consult with Yamagata on every important decision. The oligarchs were also weakened by changes within the elites. A younger generation of military officers chafed at the continuing hegemony of Satsuma and Chōshū generals and admirals. In the civil bureaucracy, younger officials who had graduated from the Law Faculty of Tokyo Imperial University were achieving positions of responsibility. Confident of their ability, they believed that governmental officials should be independent and resisted the oligarchs almost as much as they resisted the parties.

The oligarchs, nevertheless, held onto the power to act for the emperor in appointing prime ministers. After the deaths of Itō in 1909, Yamagata in 1922, and Matsukata Masayoshi (a Satsuma samurai who had been a finance minister and twice a prime minister) in 1924, this vital function was taken over by Saionji and, later, by ex-prime ministers.

As the rising and descending curves closed, the political parties made important gains. One critical turning point was in 1912. The Army withdrew its minister when its demands for a larger budget were refused; this caused Saionji's cabinet to fall. Katsura formed a new cabinet, but in place of Diet support, he tried to govern using imperial decrees. The parties were enraged and even the usually compliant Seiyūkai withdrew its support. Massive popular demonstrations broke out, a movement was hastily organized for the "Protection of the Constitution," while party orators shouted, "Destroy the Satsuma–Chōshū clique" and "Off with Katsura's head." To counter the opposition, Katsura formed a second political party that he hoped would rival the Seiyūkai. The party, later known as the Kenseikai and then the Minseitō, became important during the 1920s, but Katsura was forced to resign in 1913. The lower house had brought down a prime minister.

The two curves finally crossed in 1918, when Hara became prime minister. It was the first time that a politician who was not a Meiji founding father or a protégé of one had obtained the post. He enacted several reforms but did nothing to remedy the parliamentary shortcomings of the Meiji Constitution.

Another development was the wave of liberalism that began during World War I and reached a high tide in the period of party governments from 1924 to 1932. After Japan joined the Allies in World War I, it became increasingly influenced by democratic ideas from England and America. Scholars discussed revising the Meiji Constitution. Labor unions were organized, at first liberal and often Christian, and later Marxist. A social movement was launched to improve conditions in Japan's industrial slums and to pass social and labor legislation. Japan's second political party, the Kenseikai, out of power since 1916, grew steadily more liberal and adopted new social causes, such as universal manhood suffrage. When Hara cut the tax qualification for voting from ten to three yen—effectively enfranchising small landowners—the Kenseikai criticized the change as insufficient and accused the Seiyūkai of being "a perpetrator of class despotism."

A brief interlude of nonparty cabinets between 1922 and 1924 prompted the Kenseikai to begin a Second Movement for the Protection of the Constitution. Liberal factions of the other big party, the Seiyūkai, joined in the movement, and the two parties formed a coalition government in 1924. For the next eight years the presidents of one or another of the two major parties were appointed as prime ministers.

The cabinets (1924–1926) of Katō Kōmei are considered the peak of parliamentary government in prewar Japan. Born in 1860, Katō graduated from Tokyo Imperial University and entered the Mitsubishi combine, later marrying the boss's daughter. After studying in England, he joined the Foreign Ministry and became foreign minister at 40. For a country that esteemed age, his rise was meteoric. He subsequently became a Diet member, the president of a newspaper company, ambassador to England, and president of the Kenseikai. Outspoken, cold, and haughty, Katō was widely respected, if not liked. He was an Anglophile who understood and advocated a British model of government. His ministry passed universal manhood suffrage, increased academic appointments to the House of Peers, and cut the military budget from 42 percent in 1922 to 29 percent in 1925. He also enacted social and labor legislation. In effect, he legalized the moderate socialist movement while, at the same time, used "peace preservation" legislation to outlaw revolutionary socialism. Kato's cabinet brought Japan closer to a true parliamentary government. Political thinkers saw party cabinets as firmly established. They had not been mandated by the Meiji Constitution but neither had they been banned.

MILITARISM AND WAR (1927–1945)

Between 1890 and 1926 the political parties had been Japan's obstreperous elite. Using their legislative and budget-approval power in the Diet, they had forced other elites to compromise and had advanced to the point that party presidents were regularly named as prime ministers. During the mid-1920s the future of parliamentary government seemed assured: the economy was growing, society was stable, Japan's international position was secure. But from the 1930s the military, abetted by ultranationalists, became the new obstreperous elite, and within a decade the parties had lost most of their earlier gains. Admirals and generals replaced party presidents as prime ministers, Japan began to expand in Asia, and allying itself with Germany and Italy, it went to war with the United States in 1941. How did this come about?

The Army and Navy

Part of the answer lies in the character of Japan's military. Soldiers were not samurai. The rifle companies of Satsuma and Chōshū had broken decisively with that tradition, and universal conscription had put the new military on a changed footing. But from their inception, the military services in Japan were like separate little societies within the larger society and were constructed on different principles. They had their own schools in which students were taught the values of discipline, bravery, loyalty, and obedience. Military men saw themselves as the true guardians of Japanese tradition and as the true heirs of those who had founded the modern Japanese state. They contrasted their loyalty to the emperor and their concern for all Japanese with the pandering to special interests by the political parties.

The constitutional position of the services did not change even during the liberalism of the 1920s. Army and Navy ministers as cabinet members answered to the prime minister; but Army and Navy general staffs remained directly responsible to the emperor, and with the passing of the Meiji oligarchs, this meant that they were responsible to no one but themselves.

During the 1920s resentments rose among the military services. No longer did people speak of their glorious victories over China and Russia at the turn of the century. Year by year military budgets were cut. The prestige of a military career declined to the point that officers wore civilian clothes when not on duty. At the level of national defense policy, the fleet wing of the Navy rankled over the decision by moderate admirals to accept a formula at the 1930 London Naval Conference that would weaken Japan's naval strength.

A Crisis in Manchuria

Another part of the explanation for the rise of the military lies in the changing international order. The multilateral treaties (the 1921-22 Washington Conference and the 1930 London Conference) that replaced the earlier system of bilateral treaties (such as the Anglo-Japanese Alliance) recognized the existing colonies of the victors in World War I but opposed new colonial ventures. The Western treaty powers were especially insistent on an "open door" in China, which in their minds included Manchuria. Because Japan maintained its interests through a tame Chinese warlord, Manchuria was not, strictly speaking, a colony. But because Japan had gained its special position in Manchuria at the cost of 100,000 lives in the 1904–1905 Russo-Japanese War, it saw its claim to Manchuria as no less valid than those of Western nations to their colonies.

From the late 1920s the Kuomintang unification of China and the blossoming of Chinese nationalism threatened Japan's special position. Japanese army units stationed in south Manchuria tried to block the Nationalists' march north and murdered the Manchurian warlord when he showed signs of independence. In the face of this threat, the party government in Tokyo equivocated; it hoped to preserve the status quo even as the situation became more dire. The army saw Manchuria as a buffer between the Soviet Union and the Japanese colony of Korea and was unwilling to make concessions to the Chinese. So in 1931 local army units provoked a crisis, took over Manchuria, and proclaimed it an independent state in 1932. The government in Tokyo accepted the action, which it had not approved of beforehand. When the League of Nations—the voice of the Western colonial powers—condemned Japan for violating the "open door," Japan withdrew from the League in 1933.

The Great Depression

Just as the crisis in Manchuria called into question Japan's place in the international political order, so did the worldwide Great Depression cast doubts on the international economic order and on the *zaibatsu* at home. Critics on both the left and right condemned Mitsui, Mitsubishi, and other rich and powerful combines for profiteering at a time when the common people were deprived and suffering. In their eyes the capitalist combines were backers of the "established parties" and internationalists in an age of rising nationalism.

Rural Japan was especially hard hit. The real income of farmers fell by one third between 1926 and 1931. Our images of the Depression in Japan, not necessarily representative, come primarily from the northeast, where a crop failure led to famine in 1931. Children turned to begging for food from passing trains, tenant farmers staved off hunger by eating the inner bark of pine trees or the roots of wild plants, daughters were sold into prostitution. Urban workers suffered, too. The value of Japanese exports dropped 50 percent between 1929 and 1931. Workers' real income dropped from an index of 100 in 1929 to 69 in 1931. Unemployment rose to three million, forcing many factory workers to return to their villages and adding to the burden on the farm economy. Only the salaried middle class was better off as prices declined.

As noted earlier, the government acted effectively to counter the Depression. By 1936 Japan's heavy industries were growing apace, farmers had recovered, and workers' real wages were up. But the recovery came too late to help the political parties; by 1936 political changes begun during the worst years of the Depression had become irreversible.

The Depression galvanized both the political left and right. The political left was composed mainly of socialist moderates who won 8 Diet seats in 1928, 18 in 1936, and 37 in 1937. Supported by unionists and white-collar workers, they would reemerge as an even stronger force after World War II. There was also a splintered radical left, consisting of the Japanese Communist Party, which had been founded in

1922, and of many other little radical parties led by intellectuals. Although small and subject to growing police repression, the radical left became influential in intellectual and literary circles during the 1920s and 1930s.

The Radical Right and the Military

The political right in pre–World War II Japan is difficult to define. Most Japanese were patriotic, imbued with a strong emperor-centered nationalism. They felt no contradiction between such feelings and their support of the centrist parties in which nationalism and some measure of liberalism coexisted. During the 1930s, however, a new array of right-wing organizations went beyond the usual nationalism to challenge the status quo. Some were traditionalistic with ideologies that mixed emperorism, Shinto, and Confucian ethics. Others espoused revolutionary nationalism and argued for the "reconstruction" of Japanese society. Not a few bureaucrats looked to the example of Nazi Germany and argued for the exclusion of party politicians from government; bureaucrats could run it better, serving the interests of all the people. Military officers, with similar arguments, envisioned a "defense state" guided by themselves. They argued for military expansion and an autarchic colonial empire insulated from the uncertainties of the world economy. Young officers of the revolutionary right advocated "direct action" against the elites of the parliamentary coalition and called for a second restoration of imperial power.

It was the last group that precipitated a political crisis. On May 15, 1932, about 20 junior army and navy officers attacked the Seiyūkai offices, the Bank of Japan, and the Tokyo police headquarters, and murdered Prime Minister Inukai. The attack occurred at the peak of right-wing agitation and the pit of the depression. Given these circumstances, Saionji decided not to appoint another party president as the new prime minister and instead chose a moderate admiral. For the next four years, cabinets were led by moderate military men but with continuing party participation. These cabinets were no more than a holding pattern; they satisfied neither the parties nor the radical young officers.

During 1936 and 1937 Japanese politics were buffeted by crosscurrents but continued to drift to the right. The election of February 1936 was a victory for liberal forces in Japan. Using the slogan "What shall it be, parliamentary government or Fascism?" the Minseitō, the successor party to the Kenseikai, defeated the Seiyūkai and won control of the Diet. Barely a week later their victory was undone when young army officers stationed in Tokyo attempted a coup. Leading 1400 soldiers, they attacked government offices; killed cabinet ministers, although missing the prime minister; and occupied the Diet, Army Ministry, General Staff headquarters, and other government buildings. They urged sympathetic army superiors to form a new government. But Saionji, other men about the emperor, and the navy stood firm, and bringing in other troops, suppressed the rebellion in three days. The ringleaders were

A Call for a Taishō Restoration

The radical right in 20th-century Japan was notable for its advocacy of violent, direct action. The critique of the existing society that motivated young officers during the 1930s had already been voiced by civilian ultranationalists during the 1920s. Here is a portion of the testament of Asahi Heigo, who assassinated the head of the Yasuda cartel in 1921. He was the leader of the Righteous Corps of the Divine Land.

If these actions had been taken and a Taishō (the year period 1912–1926) Restoration had occurred, who would have ruled Japan? How much of Asahi's program was similar to that of the radical left which was emerging in Japan during the same years?

Some of our countrymen are suffering from tuberculosis because of overwork, filth, and undernourishment. Others, bereaved, become streetwalkers in order to feed their beloved children. And those who were once hailed as defenders of the country are now reduced to beggary simply because they were disabled in the wars. . . . Moreover, some of our countrymen suffer hardships in prison because they committed minor crimes under the pressure of starvation, while high officials who commit major crimes escape punishment because they can manipulate the laws.

The former feudal lords, who were responsible for the death of our ancestors by putting them in the line of fire, are now nobility and enjoy a life of indolence and debauchery. Men who became generals by sacrificing our brothers' lives in battle are arrogantly preaching loyalty and patriotism as though they had achieved the victory all by themselves.

Consider this seriously! These new nobles are our enemies because they drew a pool of our blood, and the former lords and nobles are also our foes, for they took our ancestors' lives.

My fellow young idealists! Your mission is to bring about a Taishō Restoration. These are the steps you must take:

1. Bury the traitorous millionaires.
2. Crush the present political parties.
3. Bury the high officials and nobility.
4. Bring about a universal suffrage.
5. Abolish provisions for inheritance of rank and wealth.
6. Nationalize the land and bring relief to tenant farmers.
7. Confiscate all fortunes above 100,000 yen.
8. Nationalize big business.
9. Reduce military service to one year.

These are initial steps. But the punishment of the traitorous millionaires is the most urgent of all these, and there is no way of doing this except to assassinate them resolutely.

R. Tsunoda, W. T. de Bary, D. Keene, *Sources of the Japanese Tradition* (© 1958 Columbia University Press), p. 768. Reprinted with the permission of the publisher.

---

swiftly tried and executed, and generals sympathetic to their cause were retired. On the way to his execution one radical young officer shouted, "Never trust the Imperial Japanese Army." This attempted coup was the last "direct action" taken by the radical right in prewar Japan. The officers in charge of the army purge were tough-minded technocrats, who, throughout the budget cuts of the 1920s, had advocated the further modernization of Japan's weaponry. They included General Tōjō Hideki (1884–1948), who as prime minister would lead Japan into World War II.

The suppression of army radicals did not mean the military withdrew from politics. On the contrary, the services interfered more than ever in the formation of cabinets, blocking whenever possible the appointment of party politicians or liberal bureaucrats. As a result, from 1936 on, moderate party prime ministers gave way to more outspokenly militaristic figures.

Opposition to militarism remained substantial nonetheless. In the 1937 election, the prime minister, a former general, whose political slogan was "respect the gods and honor the emperor," tried to win control of the Diet by throwing government support to the Shōwakai, a Nazi-like party. The Shōwakai performed miserably at the polls, gaining only 40 Diet seats, while the two major centrist parties, the Seiyūkai and Minseitō, which had joined in opposition to the government, won 354. The Japanese people proved more level-headed than their leaders. But the centrists' victory carried little weight, for, although a peacetime government could not rule without the Diet, the Diet could not oppose a government in wartime, and by summer of that year, Japan was at war in China.

The Road to Pearl Harbor

There were three critical junctures between the outbreak of the war with China and the Japanese attack on Pearl Harbor. The first was the decision in January 1938 to strike a knockout blow at the Nationalist (or Kuomintang) government in Nanking. The war had begun the previous year when a skirmish broke out between Chinese and Japanese troops in the Peking area and quickly spread. The Japanese army leaders disagreed among themselves on whether to continue. Many held that the only threat to Japanese interests in Korea and Manchuria was the Soviet Union and that a long war in China was unnecessary and foolish. But as Japanese armies advanced, others on the general staff argued that the only way to stop the war was to convince the Chinese Nationalists that fighting was hopeless. The latter group got its way, and the army quickly occupied most of the cities and railroads of eastern China. When the Nationalist leader Chiang Kai-shek (1887–1975) refused to give in, a stalemate ensued that lasted until 1945. China was never an active theater in the Pacific War.

The second critical decision was the signing of the Tripartite Pact with Germany and Italy in September 1940. Japan had long admired Germany, taking it as a model for its constitution, army, universities, and medical system. It had joined Germany in the 1936 Anti-Comintern Pact directed against international communism. It wanted an alliance specifically directed against the Soviet Union. Germany insisted, however, that any alliance would also have to be directed against the United States and Britain.

The Japanese would not agree; the Navy, especially, saw the American Pacific fleet as a danger and was unwilling to risk being dragged into a German war. After Japanese troops were defeated by Soviet troops in an undeclared mini-war from May to September 1939 on the Mongolian-Russian border, sentiment rose in favor of an alliance with Germany, but then Germany "betrayed" Japan by signing a nonaggression pact with the Soviet Union. Japan then decided to improve its relations with the United States but balked when America insisted that it get out of China. By the late spring of 1940 German victories in Europe—the fall of Britain appeared imminent—again led military leaders in Japan to favor an alliance with Germany.

Japan signed the Tripartite Pact with three objectives in mind: to isolate the United States; to take over the Southeast Asian colonies of Britain, France, and the Netherlands; and to improve its relations with the Soviet Union through the good offices of Germany. The last objective was reached when Japan signed a neutrality pact with the Soviet Union in April 1941. Two months later, Germany attacked the Soviet Union, without consulting its ally Japan. It compounded this second "betrayal" by asking Japan to attack the Soviet Union in the east. Japan waited and watched. When the German advance was stopped short of Moscow, Japan decided, instead, to honor the neutrality pact and turn toward southeast Asia. The decision marked, in effect, the end of Japan's participation in the Axis. Thereafter, it fought its own war in Asia. But instead of deflecting American criticism as intended, the pact, by linking Japan to Germany, led to a hardening of America's position against Japanese aggression in China.

The third and fatal decision was to go to war with the United States. In June 1940, following Germany's defeat of France, Japanese troops had moved into northern French Indochina. The United States retaliated by limiting strategic exports to Japan. When Japanese troops took southern Indochina in July 1941, the United States embargoed all exports to Japan; this cut Japanese oil imports by 90 percent, precipitating the "crisis of the dwindling stockpile." The Navy's general staff warned that oil reserves would last only two years; after that, the Navy would lose its capability to fight. Its general staff pressed for the capture of the oil-rich Dutch East Indies. But it was too dangerous to move against Dutch and British colonies in Southeast Asia with the United States on its flank in the Philippines. The Navy, therefore, advocated a preemptive strike against the United States.

For Japan, already bogged down in China, the decision was a desperate gamble. By all objective measures—steel production, oil, machine tools, heavy chemicals, and shipping—the United States was clearly stronger. The Japanese military, however, misread American statements of isolationist sentiment during 1940 and 1941 and concluded that Americans had no stomach for a drawn-out war in the western Pacific. The decision for war wagered Japan's land-based air power, shorter supply lines, and what they saw as greater willpower against American productivity. At the imperial conference where the all-or-nothing decision was taken, the navy's chief of staff compared the war with the United States to a dangerous operation that might save the life of a critically ill patient.

Tōjō Hideki (1884–1948), prime minister at the time of the attack on Pearl Harbor in 1941 and one of the chief figures in the rise of Japanese militarism. [Corbis-Bettmann]

The Pacific War

On Sunday morning, December 7, 1941, even while Japanese representatives in Washington were discussing a settlement, Japan launched an air attack on Pearl Harbor, Hawaii, the chief American naval base in the Pacific. The following day the United States declared war on Japan, Germany, and Italy. Three days later, Germany and Italy declared war on the United States. The Japanese carrier-based, surprise attack was tactically brilliant. Much of the American Pacific fleet was sunk, although the aircraft carriers, out at sea, were spared. An equally crippling blow was carried out against American air power in the Philippines. The psychological effect of these attacks was to galvanize the American public: antiwar sentiment disappeared overnight.

The potential power of the United States was enormous, but it was ill-prepared for war. Conscription had been introduced in 1940, but the Army was tiny, inexperienced, and poorly equipped. Nor was American industry geared up for war. Until the middle of 1942, Japanese victories were stunning (see Map 4-2). Troops swiftly captured Guam, Wake Island, and the Philippines, then swept through Southeast Asia. By the summer of 1942, the Japanese Empire stretched from the western Aleutian Islands southward almost to Australia, and from Burma east to the Gilbert Islands in the mid-Pacific.

The tide of war slowly turned. It took time to convert American industry to war production. The decision to defeat Germany first also slowed the pace of the Pacific

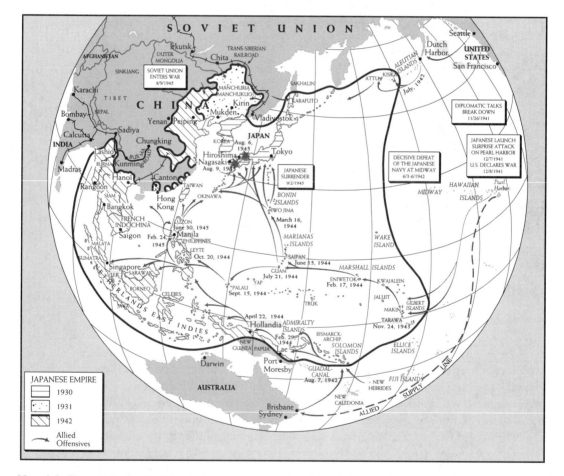

Map 4-2 The war in the Pacific. As in Europe, the Allies initially had trouble recapturing areas that the Japanese had quickly seized early in the war. The map shows the initial expansion of the Japanese and the long struggle of the Allies to push them back to their homeland and defeat them.

war. In the Battle of the Coral Sea, fought northeast of Australia in May 1942, both sides suffered equal losses, but rising U.S. ship production made such tradeoffs disadvantageous for Japan. At the Battle of Midway a month later, American planes destroyed four Japanese aircraft carriers—the core of its fleet. Thereafter Japan was on the defensive.

The original Japanese attack on the United States had been a calculated risk against the odds. The longer the war lasted, the greater the impact of American superiority in industrial production and manpower. Beginning in 1943, American forces began two campaigns of "island-hopping," selecting major bases and places strategically located along the Japanese supply lines. One campaign started in Guadalcanal in the Solomon Islands and moved north to New Guinea and the Philippines. The other moved westward across the central Pacific from the Gilberts to the Marshalls and Carolines, and then to the Marianas and Iwo Jima. The capture of Saipan and Tinian in the Marianas brought Japan within bomber range. Air raids reduced Japanese cities to ashes and industrial areas to concrete rubble and twisted girders. Dominated by the military, the Japanese government, still refused to surrender.

Confronted with Japan's determination, Americans made plans for an invasion of the Japanese homeland. But a frontal assault, they calculated, would cost unacceptable American casualties and even greater losses for the Japanese. At Okinawa more than 85 percent of the defenders had been killed and there had been more than 49,100 U.S. casualties, about one fifth at sea, where *kamikaze* suicide planes sank 34 ships and damaged 368 others. At this juncture science presented U.S. leaders with another choice: a nuclear weapon that scientists had been secretly working on since early in the war.

On August 6, 1945, an American plane dropped one of the new bombs on the city of Hiroshima. More than 70,000 of its 200,000 residents were killed. Two days later the Soviet Union declared war on Japan and hurriedly invaded Manchuria. The next day a second atomic bomb was dropped, this time on Nagasaki. An imperial conference was hastily convened to determine national policy. But even after these debacles, the opinion of the highest political and military leaders was divided: three for surrender and three for continuing the war. Emperor Hirohito (1901–1989) broke the deadlock, and Japan accepted the Allies' terms of surrender. In a radio broadcast on August 15, the emperor told the Japanese people that Japan had lost the war and that they would have to "endure the unendurable."

Japanese Militarism and German Naziism

Militarist Japan offers an interesting comparison with Nazi Germany. Both countries were late developers, with elitest, academic bureaucracies and strong military traditions. Both had paternalistic family systems. Their parliamentary systems were less

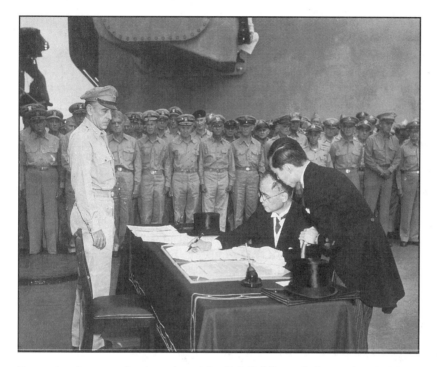

Surrender: Japanese leaders aboard the U.S.S. Missouri, September 1, 1945.
[Getty Images Inc.]

deeply rooted than those of England, France, or the United States. Stricken by the Great Depression, both sought a solution in territorial expansion and justified it in terms of being have-not nations. Both governments persecuted socialists and then liberals. In terms of their military services, communications, schools, and bureaucracies they were modern enough to implement authoritarian regimes, but their values were insufficiently modern or democratic to counter the rise of antiparliamentary forces.

The differences between the two countries are also striking. Despite the gap between its small, educated elite and the rest of the population with only a primary or middle school education, and despite the cultural split between the more Westernized cities and the more traditional rural population, Japan was more homogeneous than Germany. It had no Catholic–Protestant split. It had no powerful *Junker* class, no socialist movement that was a serious contender for political power. The political process during the 1930s was also different. In Germany parliament ruled; to come to power, the Nazis had to win an election. In this, they were helped by the combination of the Great Depression and a runaway inflation that all but destroyed the German middle class and the centrist parties along with it. In Japan's constitu-

---

MODERN JAPAN

Overthrow of Tokugawa *Bakufu*

1853–1854	Perry obtains Treaty of Friendship
1858	*Bakufu* signs commercial treaty
1861–1863	Chōshū and Satsuma mediate
1866	Chōshū defeats *bakufu* army
1868	Meiji Restoration

Nation Building

1868–1871	Shaping a new state
1871–1873	Iwakura mission
1873–1878	Social revolution from above
1877–1878	Satsuma rebellion
1881	Promise of constitution
1889	Meiji Constitution promulgated
1890	First Diet session

Imperial Japan

1894–1895	Sino-Japanese War
1900	Seiyūkai formed
1904–1905	Russo-Japanese War
1910	Korea annexed

Era of Party Government

1918	Hara becomes prime minister
1925	Katō becomes prime minister
1925	Universal manhood suffrage passed

Militarism

1931	Japan takes Manchuria
1937	War with China
1941	Japan attacks Pearl Harbor
1945	Japan surrenders

---

tional system, the Diet was weaker. Control of the government was taken away from the Seiyūkai and Minseitō even as they continued to win elections. They remained strong at the polls because Japan did not suffer from inflation and its middle class was not decimated by the Depression.

The process by which the two countries went to war was also different. In Germany the Nazis rose as a mass party, created a totalitarian state, and then made war. The Nazi Party's authority lasted until Hitler died in a Berlin bunker. In Japan there was neither a mass party nor a single group of leaders in continuous control of the government. Also, in Japan it was not the totalitarian state that made war as much as it was war that made the state totalitarian. Only after the outbreak of hostilities was the government able to implement controls over industry and begin a "spiritual mobilization" so intense that university students could be recruited as suicide *(kamikaze)* pilots.

The Allies depicted General Tōjō, who was prime minister and his own army minister during most of the war, as a Japanese Hitler. Yet when American planes began to bomb Japan in 1944, he was removed from office by the elder statesmen close to the emperor and succeeded by increasingly moderate prime ministers. The mechanisms of government of the premilitarist era still worked after a fashion. To be sure, the military continued to prosecute the war even while the government began preparations for surrender.

MODERN JAPAN IN HISTORICAL PERSPECTIVE

In the late 19th and early 20th century, Japan industrialized and was the only non-Western nation to become modern. In this regard it was closer to France, Germany, and Italy, the second-wave industrializers in Europe, than to China, India, or Turkey. Its transition to modernity may be schematized in terms of three processes: *preconditions, borrowing, and assimilation.*

The initial *preconditions* for development were the institutions and ideas in its late traditional society that served as a platform from which Japanese reached out for the ideas and insitutions of the West. Japan was fortunate in its array of preconditions. Already in place by the mid-19th century were the "Tokugawa assets" mentioned at the opening of the chapter: a fairly stable society at the "grass-roots" level; a vigorous market economy; an ethic of frugality and saving; an emphasis on education as a means of getting ahead; thinkers schooled in political philosophy; a few schools teaching Dutch and "Dutch medicine;" some sense of Japan as a nation. While not sufficient to produce an indigenous modernization, these preconditions provided an adequate base for what Natsume Sōseki characterized as an "external modernization." Among its immediate preconditions, the capacity to overthrow its ancient regime, destroy vested interests, and build a strong new state may have been critical. China during the same period had a mix of assets and liabilities not unlike those of Japan, but it lacked the readiness to topple its ancient regime and build anew.

After the 1868 Restoration, Japan eagerly *borrowed* ideas and institutions from the West. (In this, Japan was not unique. Less advanced nations in Europe borrowed from the more advanced, and the rest of the world borrowed from Europe as best it could. Borrowing advanced ideas and technology is a universal.) The process was particularly notable during the 1870s when breaks with the past were abrupt and visible. Meiji leaders established telegraph lines, post offices, banks, custom houses, hospitals, new police forces, a system of conscription, and universities with faculties of science and engineering. Japanese thinkers translated Adam Smith, Spencer, Mill, Guizot, Turgenev, and Tolstoi, and discussed at great length the applicability of their ideas to Japan. Artists began painting in oil, writers wrote political novels modeled on Victorian prototypes, and schools taught Western music and instruments. Borrowing from the West—and, more recently, contributing to it as well—has continued down to the present, at a varying pace.

Assimilation is the fusion of the borrowed with the indigenous, a process in which both the new and the old change. Western institutions were assimilated quickly, for to function they had to adapt. Banks, for instance, and particularly those banks that dealt with foreign countries, soon became almost indistinguishable from their Western counterparts. The corporate organization of the giant *zaibatsu* combines saw a greater modification of Western models to fit Japanese needs. Other cultural forms took longer to assimilate. The political novels of the 1880s were blatantly imitative of Western prototypes, the exploits of their "popular rights" heroes unbelievable in terms of normal Japanese behavior. Yet by the turn of-the-century, Japanese authors were producing serious works that were modern in their psychological depth but also true to Japanese sensibilities. Natsume Sōseki's 1911 *Kokoro* is such an example. In architecture, Victorian-style houses, red brick post offices, and granite banks early mirrored those of the West; not until after World War II would the spare beauty of Japan's traditional architecture be translated into structures of glass, steel, and concrete.

The simplicity of this schemata should not blind us to the complexity of history. The stages were neither fixed in content nor frozen in time. The preconditions in 1853, when Perry first came to Japan, had changed by the time of the Restoration in 1868. By 1881 the preconditions for an ongoing Westernization were again somewhat different; their configuration included newly assimilated Western ideas and institutions. Russia under Peter the Great, and Turkey under Ataturk, began ambitious programs of Westernization but proved unable to sustain them. In contrast, even during the 1890s and 1930s, when the pace of cultural borrowings slowed, Japan never relented in its drive for newer technologies.

As a country that experienced these stages earlier and more thoroughly, Japan may serve as a useful base for comparisons with other nations of the developing world. The field of comparative history, however, is still in its infancy.

REVIEW QUESTIONS

1. Why did the Tokugawa *bakufu* collapse as rapidly as it did? Had it been able to hang on to power, would the course of Japanese history been radically different?
2. After the Meiji Restoration, what steps did Japan's leaders take to achieve their goal of "wealth and power"?

3. Some historians, viewing development into the 1920s, regard the Meiji constitution in a positive light. Others, in view of what happened during the 1930s, see it in a negative light. Which view do you agree with, and why?

4. What led to the sudden rise of militarism during the 1930s?

SUGGESTED READINGS

G. C. Allen, *A Short Economic History of Modern Japan* (1958).

J. R. Bartholomew, *The Formation of Science in Japan* (1989). The pioneering English work on the subject.

W. G. Beasley, *Japanese Imperialism, 1894–1945* (1987). A nice description.

G. M. Berger, *Parties out of Power in Japan, 1931–1941* (1977). An analysis of political parties during the militarist era.

A. M. Craig, *Chōshū in the Meiji Restoration* (1961). A study of the Chōshū domain, the Prussia of Japan, during the period from 1840 to 1868.

A. M. Craig and D. H. Shively, eds., *Personality in Japanese History* (1970). Various authors attempt to gauge the significance of personality and the role of the individual as factors in explaining history.

P. Duus, *The Abacus and the Sword, the Japanese Penetration of Korea, 1895–1910* (1995). A nice analysis.

P. Duus, ed., Vol. 6 of *The Cambridge History of Japan: The Twentieth Century* (1988). Multi-author volume.

P. Duus, *Party Rivalry and Political Change in Taisho Japan* (1968). A study of political change in Japan during the 1910s and 1920s.

S. J. Ericson, *The Sound of the Whistle: Railroads and the State in Meiji Japan* (1996). A lively and analytical study of railroads in Japan's modernization.

Y. Fukuzawa, *Autobiography* (1966). Japan's preeminent 19th-century thinker tells of his life and of the birth of modern Japan.

S. Garon, *The State and Labor in Modern Japan* (1987).

C. N. Gluck, *Japan's Modern Myths: Ideology in the Late Meiji Period* (1988). A rich and rewarding analysis.

A. Gordon, *The Evolution of Labor Relations in Japan: Heavy Industry, 853–1955* (1985). A fine analysis of the origins of modern Japanese labor.

I. Hall, *Mori Arinori* (1973). An intellectual and political biography of Japan's first minister of education.

T. R. H. Havens, *The Valley of Darkness: The Japanese People and World War II* (1978). A social history of Japan during the war years.

A. IRIYE, *After Imperialism: The Search for a New Order in the Far East, 1921–1931* (1965). (Also read other works by the same author on Japan's international relations.)

M. B. JANSEN AND G. ROZMAN, eds., *Japan in Transition from Tokugawa to Meiji* (1986). Excellent essays on Japan's 19th-century transition by various authors.

W. JOHNSTON, *The Modern Epidemic: A History of Tuberculosis in Japan* (1995). Draws on a variety of sources—medical, social, and literary.

K. KATSU, *Musui's Story* (1988). An eminently readable autobiographical account of the life and adventures of a roisterous no-good samurai during the early 19th century.

D. KEENE, ed., *Modern Japanese Literature, an Anthology* (1960). A collection of modern Japanese short stories and excerpts from novels.

Y. T. MATSUSAKA, *The Making of Japanese Manchuria, 1904–1932* (2001).

J. W. MORLEY, ed., *The China Quagmire* (1983). A study of Japan's expansion on the continent between 1933 and 1941. (Also see other works on diplomatic history by the same author.)

R. H. MYERS AND M. R. PEATTIE, eds., *The Japanese Colonial Empire, 1895–1945* (1984).

T. NAJITA, *Hara Kei in the Politics of Compromise, 1905–1915* (1967). A study of one of Japan's greatest party leaders.

K. OHKAWA AND H. ROSOVSKY, *Japanese Economic Growth: Trend Acceleration in the Twentieth Century* (1973).

G. SHIBA, *Remembering Aizu: The Testament of Shiba Gorō* (1999). Hard times in early Meiji Japan as told by a samurai youth from a domain defeated in the Restoration wars.

E. SHIBUSAWA, *The Autobiography of Shibusawa Eiichi: From Peasant to Entrepreneur* (1994). By one of the founders of modern industry in Japan.

K. SMITH, *A Time of Crisis: Japan, the Great Depression, and Rural Revitalization* (2001). An analysis of tradition and modernity in the revitalization of rural Japan during the early thirties.

R. H. SPECTOR, *Eagle Against the Sun: The American War with Japan* (1985).

E. P. TSURUMI, *Factory Girls: Women in the Thread Mills of Meiji Japan* (1990). A work combining economic and women's history.

W. WRAY, *Mitsubishi and the N.Y. K., 1870–1914* (1984). An important study of the growth of shipping in modern Japan that also touches on the government, bureaucratic strategies, and imperialism.

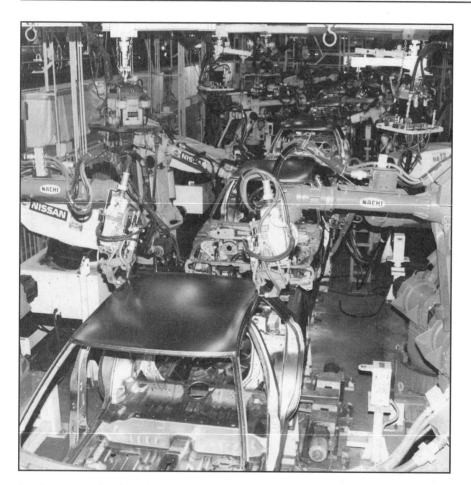

An almost completely automated assembly line at Nissan Motors' Zama factory.
The high cost of labor in Japan makes such robot-intensive production economical.
[Reuters/Susumu Takahashi/Getty Images Inc.]

chapter five

Japan, the Recent Decades

No country in the world changed so much and so quickly as Japan during the postwar decades. It repudiated wartime militarism and welcomed the reestablishment of parliamentary democracy. Its electoral politics became vigorous and free, and human rights were upheld by law, though from 1955 a single party was continuously in power. Political change was more than matched by economic growth based on a combination of free enterprise and state guidance. In the space of a single lifetime, Japanese moved from the misery and poverty of the war's aftermath to a European level of prosperity. Comparable transformations took place in society and culture. There were imbalances, to be sure, but even critics conceded that the system worked. In the early 1990s, however, the economic bubble burst, leadership failed, and a malaise gripped society. As growth almost halted, institutions that earlier had appeared exemplary were called into question and Japanese self-confidence sagged. Though Japan remained the second largest economy in the world with a stable society and an enormous pool of human talents, future problems loomed large.

THE POSTWAR OCCUPATION AND YOSHIDA SHIGERU, 1945–1954

During the first postwar decade, Japan was primarily shaped not by the American Occupation but by continuities within its own society. Its people were stoical in the face of hardship and industrious, families were stable, society was orderly. An infrastructure of schools and political, corporate, and financial institutions was in place. Prime Minister Yoshida Shigeru, in office for most of the decade, represented continuity with a conservative but nonmilitaristic past and a willingness to accommodate changes for the sake of Japan's future. Occupation reforms built on these continuities; they succeeded because they were constructive and because the Japanese people were ready for change. But among the reforms, it must also be emphasized, were some that would never have taken place had Japan not fallen briefly under foreign control.

The American Occupation

The Japanese expected a harsh and vindictive occupation. When they found it beneficent, they turned to positive cooperation. As one scholar put it, they "embraced defeat." Their disavowal of militarism and their receptivity to new democratic ideas

The Occupation of Japan

There are occupations, and then there are occupations. Former Prime Minister Yoshida Shigeru presents his view:

Is this an objective appraisal, or an attempt by Yoshida to justify his own role in the Allied Occupation?

There are some now in Japan who point to similarities between the Allied, and predominantly American, Occupation of Japan, and our Occupation of Manchuria, China and other countries of Asia—the idea apparently being that, once an Occupation régime has been established, the relationship between victors and vanquished is usually found to be the same. I regret that I cannot subscribe to this opinion. Japan's Occupation of various Asian countries,

carried out by Army officers of no higher rank than colonel and more often by raw subalterns, became an object of hatred and loathing among the peoples of the occupied countries, and there is none to dispute that fact. The Americans came into our country as our enemies, but after an Occupation lasting little less than seven years, an understanding grew up between the two peoples which is remarkable in the history of the modern world.

Criticism of Americans is a right accorded even to Americans. But in the enumeration of their faults we cannot include their Occupation of Japan.

led another scholar to label this era "the second opening of Japan." During the immediate postwar decade the primary engine of change was the Occupation, with its goal of remaking Japan.

General Douglas MacArthur (1880–1964) was the Supreme Commander for the Allied Powers (SCAP) in Japan. His headquarters in Tokyo was staffed almost entirely by Americans, and the occupation forces themselves were American, apart from British Commonwealth troops on the island of Shikoku. The chief concern of the first phase of the occupation was demilitarization and democratization. Civilians and soldiers abroad were repatriated to Japan and the military was demobilized. Ultranationalist organizations were dissolved and the Home Ministry was abolished. The police were decentralized and political prisoners freed. Following the model of the Nuremberg trials in Germany, wartime leaders were brought to trial for "crimes against humanity." Added to this, 210,000 officers, businessmen, teachers, and officials—the leaders of wartime Japan—were removed from office. The thoroughness of the dismantling of old institutions reflected the Occupation view that Japanese society had been tainted by feudal and militaristic values and that Japan's leaders had been joined in a huge conspiracy to wage aggressive war.

As a part of democratization, Shinto was disestablished as the state religion, labor unions were encouraged, and the holding companies of *zaibatsu* combines were dissolved. The old educational system, which had forced students at an early age to choose either an elite or a mass track, was changed to a single-track system that kept open longer the option of continuing in school. The most radical undertaking was a land reform that expropriated landlord holdings and sold them to landless tenants at a fractional cost. The effect, ironically, was to create a countryside of politically conservative small farmers.

Needless to say, some of these reforms merely accelerated changes already underway in Japan, and all of them depended on the cooperation of Japanese officials—in turn enthusiastic and reluctant. The Japanese officialdom had been powerful during the prewar and wartime eras; it continued so after the war, since Occupation governance was indirect. Because few Americans could speak Japanese, SCAP issued orders in English to the Liaison Bureau (the former Foreign Ministry), which then transmitted them to the appropriate Japanese ministry. (In Germany, in contrast, the Allies governed directly.)

Of all the Occupation reforms, none was more important than the new constitution, hurriedly written by the Government Section of MacArthur's headquarters and passed into law in 1947 by the Japanese Diet. It fundamentally changed Japan's polity in five respects:

1. A British-style parliamentary state was established in which the cabinet became a committee of the majority party or coalition in the Diet. This broke with the Meiji Constitution, which had permitted the emperor or those who acted in his name to appoint prime ministers without regard for the Diet. The new constitution also added an American-style independent judiciary and a federal system of prefectures with elected governors and local leaders.

2. Women were given the right to vote.

3. The rights to life, liberty, the pursuit of happiness, a free press, and free assembly were guaranteed. These were joined by newer rights such as academic freedom, collective bargaining, sexual equality in marriage, and minimal standards of wholesome and cultural living.

4. Article 9, the no-war clause, stipulated, "The Japanese people forever renounce war as a sovereign right of the nation" and will never maintain "land, sea, and air forces" or "other war potential." This article made Japan into something unique in the world: a major world power without commensurate military strength.

5. The constitution defined a new role for the emperor as "the symbol of the state deriving his position from the will of the people with whom resides sovereign power."

The Japanese people accepted the new constitution and welcomed democracy with uncritical enthusiasm. Most viewed the no-war clause as a guarantee of a peaceful future. Although it did not preclude the formation of a Self-Defense Force, it acted as a brake on military expenditures, which half a century later were only about one percent of Japan's gross domestic product. The Japanese had been readied for the changed status of the emperor by his speech on January 1, 1946, in which he renounced all claims to divinity. The Occupation saw to it that the emperor traveled about Japan in a manner appropriate to his new status as a symbol of the state. No one who saw this

Women, newly enfranchised, voting in postwar Japan.
[UPI/Corbis-Bettmann]

Two Views of the "Symbol Emperor"

The murkiest aspect of Japan's prewar emperor-centered ideology was the juxtaposition of the emperor as a modern monarch and the emperor as a living deity, ultimately descended from the sun goddess. In the first selection, former Prime Minister Yoshida Shigeru, a product of Meiji Japan, basically accepts the prewar ideology, but argues that because in fact the emperor exercised little power before World War II, nothing was changed by the postwar constitution. In the second selection, Nobel Prize winner Ōe Kenzaburō, a humanistic and slightly leftist novelist, recognizes that the emperor has been stripped of his former authority but worries about a revival of his Shinto identity.

What does Yoshida mean by "as naturally," and why does Ōe call the prewar emperor an "absolute ruler?"

1.

In regard to the question of the Imperial structure of government, as it existed in Japan, I pointed out that the Meiji Constitution had originated in the promises made to the Japanese people by the Emperor Meiji at the beginning of his reign, and there was little need to dwell on the fact that democracy, if we were to use the word, had always formed part of the traditions of our country, and was not—as some mistakenly imagined—something that was about to be introduced with the revision of the Constitution. As for the Imperial House, the idea and reality of the

mild, rumpled-looking, inarticulate man would suspect him of being a Shinto god. By the late 1960s most, though not all, Japanese had come to feel a measure of affection for Emperor Hirohito, who, they felt, had shared in their wartime and postwar hardships. They were saddened by his death in 1989. Whether the Occupation would have been wiser to abolish the emperor institution is still an open question; at the time it was felt that using him would make the job of occupying Japan easier.

By the end of 1947, most of the planned reforms had been carried out. To create the conditions in which the new democracy could take root and flourish, the Occupation in its second phase turned to Japan's economic recovery. It dropped plans to deconcentrate big business further, encouraged the Japanese government to curb inflation, and cracked down on Communist unions that used strikes for political ends. The United States also gave Japan $2 billion in economic aid.

The outbreak of the Korean War in 1950 marked the start of the third and final phase of the Occupation. The American military, fully engaged in the peninsular war, no longer had time for Japan. Consequently, Japanese officials began to look to the Cabinet and the Diet for policy decisions. By the time Japan regained its

Throne had come into being among the Japanese people as naturally as the idea of the country itself; no question of antagonism between Throne and people could possible arise; and nothing contained in the new Constitution could change that fact. The word "symbol" had been employed in the definition of the Emperor because we Japanese had always regarded the Emperor as the symbol of the country itself—a statement which any Japanese considering the issue dispassionately would be ready to recognize as an irrefutable fact.

2.

Japan's emperor system, which had apparently lost its social and political influence after the defeat in the Pacific War, is beginning to flex its muscles again, and in some respects it has already recouped much of its lost power—with two differences: first, the Japanese today will not accept the prewar

ideology-cum-theology that held the emperor to be both absolute ruler and living deity. Nevertheless, imperial rites performed quite recently were done in such a manner as to impress upon us that the emperor's lineage can be traced to a deity; I am referring here to the rituals associated with the present emperor's enthronement and the so-called Great Thanksgiving Service that followed it. These ceremonies provoked little objection from either the government or the people, indeed most Japanese seemed to take it all very much for granted.

1. *The Yoshida Memoirs*, Yoshida Shigeru. Copyright © 1961 Heineman Books, p. 139.
2. From "Speaking on Japanese Culture Before a Scandinavian Audience," *Japan, the Ambiguous and Myself: The Nobel Prize Speech and Other Lectures by Kenzaburō Ōe.* Published by Kodansha International, Ltd., 1995. Copyright © 1992 by Kenzaburō Ōe. All rights reserved. Reprinted by permission.

sovereignty in April 1952, the effect of the changeover was hardly noticeable in the daily life of the Japanese people. On the same day as the peace treaty, Japan signed a security treaty with the United States which provided for American bases and committed the United States to Japan's defense. Although attacked by the left, the security treaty would remain the cornerstone of Japan's minimalist defense policy into the 21st century.

Yoshida Shigeru and Japan's Postwar Policy

In 1945 Japan had a parliamentary potential that harked back to the rise of party power in the Diet between 1890 and 1932. It also had an authoritarian potential compounded of the factors that had led to the rise of militarism. Had the country been occupied by the Soviet Union, the efficiency of its bureaucracy, its wartime economic planning organs, its educated and disciplined workforce, and its receptivity to change after defeat might have made Japan a model Communist state. Occupied by the

United States, the parliamentary potential reemerged. This can be seen in the electoral politics of the immediate postwar years.

The first few years saw a settling down. In the 1946 election most candidates for the lower house were new to politics and many ran as independents. By the 1947 election the prewar political parties had reclaimed the field and most candidates had a party affiliation:

1937 election:	Minseitō	Seiyūkai	Social Mass Party
	36% of vote	35%	9%

1947 election:	Democrats	Liberals	Japanese Socialist Party
	25% of vote	27%	26%

The two prewar conservative parties, the Minseitō and Seiyūkai, reemerged as the Democratic Party and the Liberal Party. The prewar Social Mass Party became the Japanese Socialist Party, and, seen by many as the antithesis of wartime militarism, it made striking gains at the polls. So fierce was the competition between the two conservative parties, a legacy of prewar politics, that in 1947 the Democrats chose to form a coalition government with the Socialists, rather than with the Liberals with whom they shared a conservative agenda. But the coalition did not work. During the six years that followed, until December 1954, Japan was governed by the ministries of Yoshida Shigeru (1878–1967).

Yoshida stands out among Japan's postwar politicians. Born in 1878, he was adopted and raised as a "young master" by a wealthy Yokohama merchant. He attended the Peers' School and the Law Faculty of Tokyo Imperial University and then entered the Foreign Ministry. Though a conservative upholder of empire, he took Britain as his model. It was from this position that he criticized Japan's demands on China during World War I, the militarism of the 1930s, and the 1936 anti-Comintern pact with Germany and Italy. He became ambassador to England in 1936—the capstone of his prewar career, and retired in 1939 at age 60. In the final year of World War II, Yoshida joined a conservative group that wanted to negotiate a peace. For this he was jailed briefly by the military police—a stroke of luck in that it enabled him to avoid the postwar purge and begin a new career as a politician. He served as foreign minister in two early cabinets, then as president of the Liberal Party, and as prime minister in 1946–1947. After the brief coalition government by Socialists and Democrats, he returned to power with the victory of the Liberals in the election of 1948.

As prime minister, Yoshida was pro-business, anti-union, and anti-Communist. Although he had no enthusiasm for the Occupation reforms, he did his duty and carried them out, calling himself a "loyal servant of the emperor." Drawing strength from his popular mandate and from Occupation backing, his style of governance was autocratic, so much so that he was known as "One-Man Yoshida." He often compared himself to the early Meiji leaders, who had built a new Japan while preserving, he felt, the best of old values.

Yoshida's foreign policy—one might call it his American policy—took shape in 1950 as the United States turned its attention to the Korean War. His primary goal was economic recovery and growth. His main fear was that Japan might be drawn into the Cold War and waste its meager resources on military spending. By avoiding this, he opined, Japan might win through diplomacy what it had lost by war. In June 1950 John Foster Dulles, the American emissary, made the first of several visits to Japan. He demanded that Japan rearm and become an ally of the United States in exchange for a peace treaty and the restoration of Japanese sovereignty. For the sake of Japan's security, Yoshida wanted the alliance. But he refused more than a token rearmament on the grounds of Japan's economic weakness and Article 9, the no-war clause in the Constitution. In the end, Dulles gave more than he got. The Mutual Security Treaty, effective in 1952, guaranteed Japan's security in return for U.S. bases in Japan. Japan also established a small military force for use solely within Japan. In 1950 it was called the National Police Reserve, and after 1954, it was known as the Self-Defense Forces.

Yoshida's concern with growth coincided with the SCAP policy shift in 1948 toward economic recovery. In 1947 Japanese production was 37 percent of prewar levels. To curb inflation, in 1949 SCAP forced Japan to adopt a politically unpopular but economically necessary austerity program. Then, during the Korean War—Yoshida called it "a gift from the gods"—Japan received $4 billion in U.S. procurement orders. This led to a surge in manufacturing. By 1955 Japan's production had regained prewar levels. In one sense the "postwar" had ended.

THE COLD WAR AND THE JAPANESE TRANSFORMATION, 1955–1989

The American-Soviet "Cold War" began after World War II and continued for more than four decades as the confrontation of two vastly different political systems. In Asia the United States had adopted a "let-the-dust-settle" policy after the 1949 Communist victory in China, but then reversed its position after the North Korea invasion of South Korea in 1950. The 1952 U.S. Security Treaty with Japan was one link in a chain of treaties between the United States and the rim nations of Asia. The United States became the protector of these nations and also the principal market for their export-led growth.

In Europe the Cold War ended with the fall of the Berlin Wall in 1989 and the collapse of the Soviet Union in 1991. In Asia the end was less clearly defined. Though the nuclear threat of the Soviet Union had ended, Communist parties still ruled in China, North Korea, and Vietnam. But as China and then Vietnam began to shift to market economies, they increasingly sought accommodation with the United States, Japan, and other non-Communist states. It was as if the kaleidoscope of foreign relations was slowly being shaken.

In the Cold War, no other developed nation played so small a role as Japan. During the 1960s, 1970s, and 1980s, the government basically continued the policies begun by Yoshida. It focused on economic growth while relying on the United States for its security; it spent less on its military than any other major power. One Japanese ex-bureaucrat even suggested that if the international system of the Cold War were seen in terms of Tokugawa class society, the United States and the Soviet Union would be samurai, Japan a merchant, and Third World nations peasants. Japan would do well, he added, to put aside higher political principles and stick to trade. Another politician said much the same thing more bluntly: "If we continue to bet on the Anglo-Saxons, we should be safe for at least twenty years."

Despite Japan's passive stance, the Cold War provided a stable framework for its development. The United States sponsored Japan's membership in GATT and other international economic organizations. It remained open to Japanese exports even during the 1950s and 1960s when Japan was still protectionist. In turn, Japan supported the United States in most areas of foreign policy. Until 1972, when President Nixon visited Peking, Japan recognized the Republic of China (that is, Taiwan), and not Peking, as the legitimate government of China. Only rarely, as in its vital relations with Middle Eastern oil-producing nations, did it follow an independent course. Leftist critics as well as some nationalists denounced the government for having no policy of its own. The centrist-conservative majority defended its policy, saying that, however passive, it fit the emphasis on economic growth and was justified by the results.

Economic Growth

After recovering to prewar levels in 1955, Japan's economic advance was expected to moderate. Instead, it forged ahead and continued to grow at a double-digit pace for nearly two decades. Shipbuilding, machine tools, steel, heavy chemicals, automobiles, consumer electronics, and optics led the way. By the 1970s, names like Sony, Toyota, Seiko, Honda, Canon, Nissan, and Panasonic were known throughout the world for the quality of their products. Though some economists spoke of this growth as miraculous, it is better seen as the consequence of a single-minded national policy summed up in the phrase "growth at any price."

A few simple figures will illustrate the magnitude of its growth. In 1955 Japan had a gross national product of $24 billion, with a per-capita product of $268; 20 years later the figures were $484 billion and $4320. By 1989, when the Cold War ended, the figures were $2,830 billion and $23,033.

The growth may be explained by a combination of factors: an infrastructure of banking, marketing, and manufacturing skills had carried over from the prewar years; a favorable international situation existed: oil was cheap, access to raw materials and markets easy. Especially important during the early decades was the openness of the U.S. market to Japanese exports; American sponsorship gained Japan early entry into the World Bank, the International Monetary Fund, and other international organizations. A savings rate close to 20 percent supported reinvestment; it reflected a traditional frugality but was also necessary to supplement inadequate pensions.

A revolution in education also contributed. Prewar education for most Japanese had ended with middle school, and only a tiny fraction attended university. By the early 1980s, almost all middle school graduates went on to high school and half of high school graduates went on to higher education, about the same as in advanced European nations. Even more telling, by the early 1980s Japan was graduating more engineers than the United States, and virtually all of them were employed in nonmilitary, productive industries. (In contrast, the total number of lawyers in Japan roughly equaled a single year's graduating class from American law schools.)

The upgrading of human capital and the channeling of its best minds into productive careers enabled Japan to tap the huge backlog of technology that had developed in the United States during and after the war years. The United States, yet to consider Japan a serious competitor, was willing to share its science and know-how. For Japan it proved far cheaper to license or buy technology than to invent it. After "improvement engineering," Japan sold its products to the world. In 1953 the company that would become Sony licensed the transistor from Western Electric for $25,000. Later, a Japanese company bought rights to the VCR, which, developed by American engineers, had been sold to film studios for thousands of dollars a unit. After reengineering, the Japanese sold huge numbers of the device to the general public for several hundred dollars a copy.

An abundance of skilled cheap labor also helped. Following a postwar baby boom, the population in 1950 reached 83 million; by 1990 it had risen to 123 million. Immediately after the war 47 percent of Japan's labor force was in agriculture, but as agriculture became more efficient, industry siphoned off excess labor, until by 2000, less than 5 percent worked on the land. During the 1950s and 1960s more labor was available than jobs, keeping wages low.

Labor organization, too, was no bar to economic growth. Industrial workers in Japan during the immediate postwar decades were more highly unionized than those in the United States, but the basic component of labor organization was the company-based union, rather than a trade union. The unions regularly engaged in spring offensives and marched with red flags on May Day, but they usually took great pains not to impair their companies' productivity. In recent decades, as in the United States and most of Europe, the strength of unions has declined as labor has become more diverse.

The government aided manufacturers with allocations of foreign exchange and special depreciation allowances. It gave industries in advanced technologies cheap loans, subsidies, and the research products of its own laboratories. Tariffs were used to protect such industries until they were secure at home and able to compete abroad. Small budgets for defense spending and welfare enabled the

Like Water Gushing from a Fountain

During the 1950s and 1960s at least, a national consensus supported economic growth. "Catch up with and pass Europe and America" was a slogan accepted by businessmen, bureaucrats, and workers alike. A banner in a rolling mill in northern Kyushu read, "Let us lead the world in quality and quantity." The words of the company song with which Matsushita (Panasonic) workers and managers greeted each new day of work during the 1960s was not atypical.

There is a paradox. On the one hand, Japanese labor during these decades was highly unionized; on May Day the workers marched with red flags; and they generally voted the socialist ticket. On the other hand, they strongly identified with their companies. They saw their personal well-being as tied up *with the fortunes of their company; and they rarely permitted strikes to interfere with production. Is the juxtaposition of such contradictory feelings a normal part of most lives? Can you imagine American, British or French workers gathering together to sing such a song at the start of each workday?*

For the building of a new Japan,
Let's put our strength and mind together,
Doing our best to promote production,
Sending our goods to the people of the world,
Endlessly and continuously,
Like water gushing from a fountain,
Grow industry, grow, grow, grow!
Harmony and sincerity,
Matsushita Electric!

government to keep corporate taxes low. The Finance Ministry and the Ministry of Trade and Industry encouraged the Bank of Japan to back private banks in refinancing Japan's industries. Critics who spoke of "Japan Inc." as though Japan were a single, gigantic corporation overstated the case. Government may have been more supportive of business than regulative, but competition between companies was nonetheless fierce. Also, government planners were sometimes wrong; they felt, for example, that Japan was too small for an automobile industry and offered no support. The private sector, ignoring government guidance, went ahead on its own. Automobile production grew from 8000 vehicles in 1953 to 3 million in 1970, to nearly 10 million in 1990, when Japan became the largest car producer in the world.

By 1973 Japan's economy had become "mature." Double-digit growth gave way to a still-respectable four percent growth. Some favorable factors continued, such as open world markets and low defense spending. But others changed. Labor became more expensive as demand outstripped supply, salaries rose, and the number of better-paid, older workers increased. The advantage of cheap labor passed to South

Korea, Taiwan, and Hong Kong. The formation of OPEC made oil more expensive. Research costs grew as the backlog of cheap technology declined. Government expenditures rose as welfare programs and tough but costly antipollution policies were implemented. As growth slowed, the composition of the economy changed: smoke stack industries declined while pharmaceuticals, specialty chemicals, scientific equipment, computers, robots, automobiles, and a variety of service industries grew.

The pattern of trade also changed markedly. Between 1955 and 1975 Japan's exports rose from $2 to $56 billion; by 1990, to $286 billion. Through the 1970s its trade was benign in the sense that exports were a smaller part of its national product than those of England, France, or Germany, and exports were balanced by imports. That trade should have balanced is not surprising, since Japan, poorly endowed with natural resources, had to import much of its food and raw materials and all of its oil. But from the 1980s, huge trade surpluses appeared. Particularly with the United States, far and away Japan's biggest market, Japan enjoyed trade surpluses of $40 to $50 billion a year. The surpluses were generated mainly by the appetite for excellent Japanese products, but they were also bolstered by protectionist policies.

In the 1960s and 1970s the world had seen Japan and Japan had seen itself as a small country that was doing well. In the 1980s a new image emerged of Japan as an economic superpower. An American sociologist wrote a book titled *Japan as Number One*, which became a best-seller in Japan. Third World nations looked to Japan as a model to emulate. Economists in Singapore spoke of an "Asian pattern of economic development" that combined a market economy with strong government guidance, high technology, education, and elements of traditional morality. Japanese self-confidence also soared as the yen rose in value and the standard of living reached European levels. Japanese scholars, reflecting a new nationalism, acclaimed Japan as an "information society," a new stage of civilization that went beyond earlier Western models.

During the 1980s some saw Japan as unique within the capitalist world. American magazines often asked whether it was possible for others to compete against Japan's state-protected free enterprise system. When American officials complained of the unfavorable balance of trade and asked for an "even playing field," Japanese officials advised them to "put their own house in order." As Japanese self-confidence peaked, a prominent politician wrote a book, *The Japan That Can Say No*. He omitted "to the United States" from the title, but that was understood. A columnist, commenting on drugs and crime in America, wrote in the *Asahi* newspaper: "Watching the United States suddenly losing its magnificence is like watching a former lover's beauty wither away. It makes me want to cover my eyes." Believing their boom would never end, Japanese bid up the prices of corporate shares and land to several times the European and American levels. The Tokyo Dow rocketed from less than 13,000 in 1985 to almost 39,000 four years later, and real estate rose almost as much. The value of the yen doubled in three years.

Society

As a complex modern society, Japan is not easily summed up in a few para-graphs. One important change was urbanization: at war's end almost half of all Japanese lived in the countryside, but by 1989 most lived in cities, almost one quarter in the Tokyo-Osaka corridor. Within cities population shifted from more traditional small industries characterized by long hours, low pay, and few benefits to modern industries with shorter work hours, higher pay, and more benefits, including the secu-rity of lifetime employment—although even in the modern sector, part-time employees and temporary workers were paid less and given fewer benefits. There also began a shift from manufacturing to service industries.

Families changed. In the prewar period the three-generation extended family of grandparents, parents, and children was considered standard. By the early postwar period the nuclear family of parents and children was the norm and the extended family was seen as old-fashioned. When husbands and wives left the countryside to work in new industries, they left grandparents behind. By the late 1960s the two-child family had become the ideal; by 2000 woman of childbearing age had an average of only 1.33 children. Companies and government offices in the 1950s and 1960s built huge apart-ment complexes on the edges of cities for their employees. Wives, particularly, wel-comed life in the tiny apartments without mother-in-laws. During the 1960s and 1970s larger apartments, called "mansions" in Japanese, were built in cities and purchased by middle- and higher- income families. Only the rich could buy city houses. As standards of living rose, the apartments became filled with rice cookers, washing machines, dryers, televisions, computers, and electronic equipment. Consumerism was constrained only by the small size of the living units and the impossibly high prices of real estate.

The status and condition of women rose. Occupation reforms had given women the right to vote, legal equality, and an equal share of the family inheritance. Women's colleges gained the right to award degrees, and women began to enter hitherto all-male universities, including the eight former imperial universities. Rising incomes and smaller families enabled parents to give all of their children a higher education. Dating and coed excursions to ski slopes or ocean beaches became commonplace. Arranged marriages declined precipitously, and the "love" marriage became the norm.

Most women worked for a while after completing their education and before mar-riage, and they married later. They usually chose to stay at home while their children were small, but many returned to work when their children entered middle school. With the shift toward nuclear families, wives became the household authority figure, at least during the long hours that their husbands worked and commuted. Family outings became a common sight in parks, shrines, and other public places. Slowly rising divorce rates reflected the growing economic independence of women. As a sign of the times, female workers in Japanese offices sometimes refused to serve tea, and there was a rising number of legal suits related to *sekuhara*—sexual harassment. Still, the feminist movement was weaker in Japan than in the West. Japanese feminists pointed out the small number of women in the Diet and high-level positions in business and government.

Rising educational levels also led to social change. Getting ahead depended on education. Students were under enormous pressures to enter good schools from kindergarten on. Mothers routinely compared children's test scores. "Education mommas" even sent their grade-school children to afterschool tutoring classes. Examinations controlled admissions at every level, even for the numerous cram schools that prepped failed candidates to retake the university entrance examinations. Magazine articles routinely lamented the excesses of Japan's "examination society," but few steps were taken to remedy them. Most students realized that the pressure to excel was for their own good, and limited their rebellion to reading violent and sadistic *manga*, though a few rebelled openly.

On the positive side, the enormous prewar gap between the tiny educated elite and the masses with only a middle school education disappeared. Because virtually all Japanese, rich and poor alike, were at least high school graduates, they tended to see themselves as middle class. This consciousness was the social base for Japan's parliamentary democracy, especially for the growing number of voters who described themselves as "independents." It also provided the market for Japan's tremendous output of newspapers, magazines, and books. Bookstores stocked every variety of books imaginable: serious fiction, detective stories, histories, poetry, science fiction, romances, cookbooks, translations of foreign works, as well as books on investing, self-improvement, and home repairs.

In prewar Japan the claims of the individual vis-à-vis the family, community, and state were often weak. In the postwar era, economic prosperity brought greater personal autonomy. Public opinion polls of the young revealed a desire for more meaningful work and a sphere of independence apart from work. Small pleasures did not replace duties but became an expected part of everyday life. The young took affluence for granted and met with friends at Kentucky Fried Chicken, MacDonalds, or one of their many Japanese imitators. They went to coffee houses, read *manga*, and watched American movies and Japanese *animé*.

Women may have gained more than men. In the newly extended interim between school and marriage, they arrived at a measure of self-realization. The sentimental verse of Tawara Machi's best-selling *Salad Anniversary* reflects the self-oriented and nonideological individualism that began in the late postwar era.

The girl had a boyfriend:

Rattling me along
to where you wait in Shinjuku
the Odakyu Line is my Silk Road . . .

Secretly I try on your jacket
drinking in your smell
and strike a pose like James Dean . . .

May of my twenty-first year—
the word "motherhood"
a pure abstraction

Like 100% juice
from finest Valencia oranges,
unstrained

Sunday morning—
in sandals, we set off together
to shop for bread and beer. . . .

Breaking up, she is once more alone. Will she stay at home or live in Tokyo?

Caught between two choices
I lie spread-eagled—
in perfect bilateral symmetry . . .

She decides.

The day I left for Tokyo
Mother looked older by all the years
of separation ahead

Fukui Station, where I left Mother
with a light "See you then"—
as if going shopping . .

The city is impersonal.

Beautician who's cut my hair three times
asks me as I take my seat
"Is this your first time here?"

She visits her parents,

In my hometown, children's boots
running in the snow
like a sprinkling of bright gumdrops . . .

From mother-and-daughter
we turn into a pair of women
an age when I think of marrying

and then returns to Tokyo.

> Groping in the mailbox
> of my solitary room—
> already my face has back its Tokyo feel.[1]

During the early decades, serious social problems also arose. Growth at any price led to tragic incidents of cadmium and mercury poisoning. Air pollution affected major cities. But before opposition parties could seize on the issue, stringent new laws were passed and enforced. During the late 1950s Fujimibashi, the Tokyo "bridge from which Mount Fuji can be seen," was a misnomer, but by the early 1970s Fuji was again visible on clear days.

In the early postwar years, welfare programs were minimal or nonexistent. The care of the poor, old, sick, orphaned, and mentally troubled fell mainly on families and relatives. During the 1970s and 1980s programs grew, and by the early 1990s high-quality programs had become fairly substantial at city, prefectural, and national levels.

Attitudes toward minorities, perhaps two percent of the population, also improved during these years. The Ainu of Hokkaido, long despised and neglected, had mostly died off or been absorbed into the majority population during the prewar century. In the postwar years, the few tens of thousands that survived formed political organizations to protect themselves and spoke of maintaining a separate cultural identity. Supported by the political left, they obtained favorable legislation and their condition improved. A larger problem was the *burakumin*, or members of outcast communities—a legacy of the Tokugawa era, who were especially numerous in western Japan. Though physically indistinguishable from other Japanese, their members were shunned as marriage partners and frequently barred from good jobs. In some areas parents hired detectives to check the antecedents of their children's potential spouses. Though prejudice against the group diminished among the postwar generation, the problem persisted. A still more intractable problem was the 900,000 Koreans in Japan. By the 1980s most had been born in Japan and had a Japanese education but were not citizens, since citizenship was determined by blood, not birthplace. As South Korea industrialized, Koreans in Japan were no longer seen as citizens of a backward nation, but they were still viewed as separate from the Japanese and suffered social and occupational prejudices.

Politics

Japanese politics between 1955 and 1993 has been described as the "one and a half party system." The one party was the Liberal Democratic Party (LDP), formed

---

[1]Tawara Machi (J. W. Carpenter, trans.), *Salad Anniversary* (1989), pp. 89–90, 93, 143–144, 146–147, 156–158.

by a merger of the two conservative parties in 1955. It held power throughout this period. The "half party," so called because it was permanently out of power, was the Japanese Socialist Party. The left and right wings of the socialists had split into two parties in 1951 but rejoined in 1955.

One-party rule is not usually associated with representative government. What did it mean for Japan to have one-party rule for 38 years? The LDP stayed in power by winning elections, which were open, fair, orderly, and marked by vigorous campaigning. In the immediate postwar years, the conservatives' strength at the polls was simply the continuation of prewar constituencies: the networks of ties between communities, local men of influence, prefectural assemblymen, and Diet politicians, and their ties to business and the bureaucracy. From the 1960s onward, the LDP became identified in the public mind as the party that was rebuilding Japan and maintaining Japan's security through close ties with the United States. It was widely recognized as the party of ability. Despite the cozy relationships that developed between the LDP and business, periodic scandals, and a widespread distrust of politicians, it stayed in power, election after election. Rule by a single party for such a long period provided for an unusual continuity in government policies.

In the Japanese context "conservative" means some of the same things it might mean in the West: the LDP was pro-business, anti-Communist, opposed to inflation, and more inclined than its opposition to uphold traditional values. But the LDP was very different from, say, the Republican Party in the United States. It was protectionist toward Japanese agriculture and new, cutting-edge industries; it favored bureaucratic guidance of the economy; and it never even considered permitting civilians to own guns or revising the lenient laws on abortion.

Within the larger pattern of the LDP hegemony, several trends were notable:

1. From 1955 to 1960, Japanese politics was marked by ideological strife. The LDP was led by wartime figures who had been purged after the war but had resumed their political careers. These leaders rather high-handedly modified several Occupation reforms, recentralized the police, strengthened central government controls over education, and even considered a revision of the Constitution. The opposition was led by Marxist socialists, many of whom had been persecuted during the war. The Socialists branded LDP governance as the "tyranny of the majority," since legislation was often passed by "snap votes," and warned of the revival of authoritarianism. Diet sessions were marked by confrontation, rancor, and occasional violence.

    After 1960 confrontation gradually declined. A new generation of leaders who cared less about the battles of the past came to the fore. Adopting a "low posture," the new LDP prime minister dropped controversial political issues and drew up a plan to double the national income in ten years. These moves inaugurated a more peaceful era. As prosperity grew during the 1970s and 1980s, ideological confrontation declined further. The revolutionary left within the Socialist

Party became weaker, as did the traditionalist right in the LDP. In many areas a consensus emerged as the LDP consulted opposition politicians and obtained their support before presenting new bills to the Diet.

2.   Another trend was a steady decline in the LDP popular vote from 63.2 percent in 1955 to 54.7 percent in 1963, to 42.7 percent in 1976. The decline mirrored Japan's economic growth: farmers, fishermen, small shopkeepers, and the self-employed who traditionally voted for the LDP became a smaller part of the population, while unionized laborers and white-collar workers, who tended to vote for the socialists, increased. By the mid-1970s, the conservatives faced the possibility that they would soon have to form a coalition to stay in power. Political commentators spoke of the dawning of "an age of parity." But in 1979 the steady 20-year decline in the LDP popular vote came to an end. Some white-collar workers and the better-paid elite among unionized workers began to vote for the LDP. Also, unionization of the work force declined from a high of 46 percent in 1950 to half that figure during the 1980s. For the next 14 years the LDP enjoyed a stable majority in the powerful lower house of the Diet—though not always in the upper house—and remained in power.

3.   Even though it received less than half of the popular vote, the LDP maintained its Diet majority because its opposition became fragmented. In 1960 non-Marxist members broke from the Socialist Party, the principal opposition party, to form a competing Democratic Socialist Party. In 1964 the Value Creating Society (*Sōka Gakkai*), a Nichiren Buddhist sect that grew to include almost one tenth of the Japanese population, formed the Clean Government Party (*Kōmeitō*). The Japanese Communist Party, which had become militant and lost votes during the Korean War, broke with the Soviet Union and presented itself as a party upholding national interests. In the 1970s and 1980s it received almost ten percent of the popular vote. During elections, these smaller opposition parties competed against each other as well as against the LDP within Japan's small election districts; the divided opposition vote benefited candidates of the larger LDP, enabling it to maintain its grip on the Diet.

THE RECENT YEARS, 1990 TO THE PRESENT

Japan's stellar performance during the earlier postwar decades dimmed as the century approached its end and the new millennium dawned. The economy turned down; politics was marked by a clear failure of leadership; and new social problems arose. Was the system broken and in need of fundamental change, the Japanese asked themselves, or was it simply that its parts were out of kilter and needed to be set aright?

A Recession Economy

Between 1989 and 1992 the Japanese "bubble" burst. Land prices dropped, and corporate shares plummeted to about one third of their former value. Japanese who owned shares or who had bought property at sky-high prices felt poorer. Banks that had made housing or margin loans were left with billions of dollars worth of nonperforming loans. Both banks and individuals retrenched, further slowing the economy. Many small and a few larger companies went bankrupt; others were forced to restructure, cut their research budgets, and lay off workers or nudge them into early retirement. Companies also hired fewer new graduates. Unemployment rose from less than two to four and then to more than five percent, and hidden unemployment was considerably higher. All these problems were exacerbated by the pan-Asian recession that began in 1997.

Weak government finances added to the problem. Postwar governments accustomed to deficit spending had always been bailed out by economic growth. But as the economy stalled, deficits soared. By 2000 the national debt was 136 percent of the national product, higher than in any other developed nation. Conservative governments, assuming that their "system" was sound, tried to spend their way out of the recession with expensive, and often unnecessary, public works projects. But the spending was offset by consumers, who, uncertain of the future, cut back on spending and increased their savings. The recession continued into the early years of the new century.

The seriousness of the recession and the attendant widespread pessimism must not blind us, however, to underlying strengths in the Japanese economy. Some automobile and electronic companies increased both production and exports. Japan continued to enjoy a huge surplus in its trade with the United States—in 2000, over $70 billion. With over a trillion dollars invested abroad, in 2000 Japan was the world's top creditor nation. Its labor force, while costly, was disciplined, educated, and highly skilled; managerial skills were widespread. Some Japanese manufacturing skills even seemed exportable: Nissan's plant in Tennessee took 17.37 hours to assemble an automobile; at General Motors' plants the average was 26.75 hours. Government and private companies invested heavily in industries of the future such as airplanes, electronics, robotics, medical instruments, flat screens, nanotechnology, materials technology, and biotechnology. During the 1990s Tokyo University built huge new science and engineering buildings that dwarfed the low, prewar brick buildings of the faculties of law, letters, economics, and education. In most respects Japan's economic infrastructure held up.

The economic weight of Japan's economy also remained prodigious. Japan continued to be the second largest economy in the world, slightly larger than the combination of Germany, Britain, and France, which rank as third, fourth, and fifth, respectively. The following tables point out both Japan's size and the income level of its citizens.

A Comparison of Japan with Germany, Britain, and France, Projected 2000 Figures

	GDP (in billions)	Population (in millions)	Per-Capita GDP
Germany	$1,867	82	$22,768
Britain	1415	60	23,583
France	1,281	59	21,711
	$4,563	201	$22,701 (average)
Japan	$4,614	126	$36,619

To be sure, food and clothing are so expensive in Japan that the per-capita product sounds better than it is. Furthermore, any comparison fluctuates year to year with the exchange rates of currencies.

Just as telling is a comparison with other Asian nations (taken from another database).

Gross Domestic Products of Japan and Other Asian Countries (in Billions of Dollars) in the Year 2000

China (incl. H.K.)	$1,265	Japan	$4,759
South Korea	457		
Taiwan	310		
Singapore	91		
Thailand	119		
Malaysia	89		
Indonesia	153		
Philippines	75		
Bangladesh	37		
Myanmar	6		
India	473		
Pakistan	63		
Sri Lanka	16		
Australia	380		
New Zealand	48		
Russia	251		
Total	$3,833	$4,759	

A New Age of Politics

Politics also took a sharp turn during the 1990s. For 50 years the Japanese Socialist Party had been the principal opposition party, but in the 1993 election it dropped from 136 to 70 seats in the Diet. The end of the Cold War, the worldwide rejection of Marxist ideology, the decline of labor union membership and militancy, and the widespread Japanese view that socialist politicians had little to contribute to their recession-ridden country signaled the demise of socialism in Japan. This was confirmed in 1994, when the party, hungry for a taste of power after decades in the wilderness, gave up its principles and joined the Liberal Democratic Party in a coalition government. The electorate responded in the 1996 general election by giving the socialists only 26 seats in the lower house, and in 2000, only 19 of the 480 seats. The Japanese Communist Party declined from 26 to 20 seats.

The decline of the left inaugurated a new era of multiparty conservative politics. The LDP remained the largest party, but its main opposition was now a number of smaller conservative parties. The LDP, as before, was an aggregate of factions, each with a leader and members. The smaller conservative parties usually consisted of single factions, which joined at times to form a larger party.

Japanese electoral politics during the 1990s was punctuated by scandals and factional strife, but the central issue was the economy. In the 1993 election, the LDP lost 52 of its 275 seats in the lower house of the Diet—a punishment for not having ended the recession. In its place, non-LDP coalition governments ruled from 1994 to 1996. The LDP bounced back in the 1996 election; Japanese voters increased their support in the hope that its politicians would be more effective than the less seasoned leaders of the previous coalitions. Since then, the LDP has been the dominant member of successive coalition governments. But when it became clear that the LDP policy of public works spending had failed to revitalize the economy, it dropped from 271 to 233 seats in the 2000 general election.

In a 2001 public opinion poll, 40 percent of respondents said they were dissatisfied with their lives—20 percent more than in 1998; 57 percent said they were cutting expenses in order to save more; and 87 percent called Japan's economic situation bad. Unalarmed by the 40 percent figure, some editorialists said that 60 percent were still likely to support the status quo. Some interpreted the frugally minded 57 percent as an indication of fears and uncertainty about the future. Others opined that the 87 percent figure gave a more accurate picture of national feelings.

Fearing further losses in the upper house election of July 2001, the LDP chose Koizumi Junichirō as the new prime minister in April 2001. His slogan was "Reform the party, reform Japan." His cabinet contained younger and vigorous

Map 5-1 Japan is a rich island nation surrounded by poorer but powerful neighbors. Russia is a nuclear power of the first order. China is a medium-sized nuclear power with a growing economy and rapidly modernizing military. Two areas of the world in which trouble could easily occur are also nearby: Taiwan to the south and the two Koreas to the west. For its security, Japan relies on the "nuclear umbrella," which the United States has provided since 1952. The Security Treaty with the United States is the basis for all defense planning in Japan. If it were to come to an end, a very unlikely prospect, Japan would transform itself into a nuclear power almost overnight.

Prime Minister Junichiro Koizumi. [Photo: Koji Sasahara. AP/Wide World Photos]

figures, including a woman as foreign minister. He proposed to abolish LDP factions, which voters applauded, to reform the economy, which all agreed was necessary, and to revise the Constitution in order to legalize Japan's military forces. He also supported popular causes such as fairer election districts and compensation for leprosy patients who had been unnecessarily confined. Youthful in appearance, dapper, with longish hair and a ready smile, his popularity reached an unprecedented high of 85 percent (versus 7 percent for his predecessor) and schoolgirls collected his campaign posters.

But Koizumi and his party faced a dilemma: the short-term political costs of basic reform were likely to be great. Financial bureaucrats recoiled at the cost of refinancing huge bank debts in the face of an already seriously unbalanced budget. Banks wanted to call bad debts before they grew worse but were aware that doing so would lead to new bankruptcies and higher unemployment. Raising taxes to overcome government deficits would cause pain and only deepen the recession. In the opinion of some Japanese political scientists, any fundamental reform, whatever its long-term benefits, would unseat the party that carried it out.

Another feature of the 1990s was the disproportion between Japan's economic weight and its voice in international affairs. This was partly because its military was small with only defensive capabilities; partly because its interests generally paralleled those of the United States, whose lead it continued to follow; and partly because of its brutal wartime legacy, which handicapped its relations with other East Asian nations. Those relations were certainly not helped when Koizumi's predecessor, obtuse as well as unpopular, claimed that "Japan was a divine nation centered on the emperor." Adding to these factors was Japan's preoccupation with internal problems; one columnist described Japanese foreign policy as nearly paralyzed. Many in Japan worried about the rapid strengthening and modernization of China's military and of China's growing influence on neighboring Asian nations. Japan's 1999 defense guidelines called for greater cooperation with the United States in the event of regional military crises, though any substantial cooperation was prohibited by its "peace constitution." Japan remained wary of any involvement in the defense of Taiwan.

Society, Problems, and Prospects

At the dawn of the new millennium, Japanese society had both problems and strengths. The triple vectors of change in the postwar era had been Occupation reforms, economic growth, and a rapid expansion of secondary and higher education. Taken together, one might expect them to have produced deep cultural and social dislocations. At the margin, these did occur. Villagers who migrated to the cities often felt adrift. Sometimes they joined "new religions," such as the Value Creating Society, in an attempt to recreate a sense of community. In 1995 one aberrant and apocalyptic cult released nerve gas in a Tokyo subway, leaving the Japanese shocked that something so "un-Japanese" could happen. (Small ideological groups in Japan, like the young officers' cliques in the 1930s or the Red Army Faction among students in the 1960s, have often displayed a potential for violent "direct action.")

Schools were another problem. Educators and economists agreed that Japan's lockstep primary and secondary education were appropriate to the requirements of assemblyline mass production, but questioned whether they would produce the individuality and creativity required for the new "age of information." Will Japan produce entrepreneurs like Bill Gates, they asked. Others countered that Japanese companies had displayed marvelous creativity in engineering, if not always in basic science. Sony, with its Trinitron television tube, Walkmans, CDs, and Vaio laptops, was but one example. They argued that banking reform to make venture capital available was more important than changes in schooling.

Another prominent topic in newspapers and magazines concerned bullying in schools and a surge in teenage crime. One editorialist coined the phrase "seventeen— a dangerous age." Teachers contended that moral standards ought to be taught at home, and agreed with the outspoken and nationalistic governor of Tokyo who put the blame for children's misdeeds on "the self-centered lifestyles of parents." But parents often blamed the schools and a few demanded that "moral education," banned since World War II, be reintroduced.

The most serious social problem in Japan today is the aging of its population. In 1980 there were five workers for every retired person; by 2010 and for several decades thereafter, there will be fewer than two. Corporate pensions are underfunded, private savings are inadequate, and government pensions and public pensions (the Japanese equivalent of Social Security) add to government deficits. Magazines constantly ask how will the old be supported or how will they vote in elections. This problem is not unique to Japan. In all developed nations a shift has occurred from high fertility and high mortality to low fertility and low mortality. But the imbalance is particularly severe in Japan and Germany, due to wartime population losses and the postwar baby boom that skewed the distribution of age groups.

Some see today's low birthrate as an opportunity to reduce population. Japan is crowded and would be far more liveable with fewer people. The problem of an insufficient labor force might be addressed by raising the retirement age, starting pensions later, and tapping the reservoir of nonworking, middle-aged women. Ironically, though, in recession Japan, where graduates have trouble finding jobs and companies already carry excess workers, the immediate problem is too few jobs, not too few workers.

Despite these problems, the strengths of Japanese society are considerable. The ability of the society—the family, school, office, and workshop—to absorb strains and lend support to the individual is impressive. Lifetime employment, thus far only slightly dented by the "bursting of the bubble," gives both regular workers and salaried employees a sense of security, though temporary and part-time workers remain unprotected. Polls and statistics suggest that most families are in good condition. While divorce rates are rising, they are less than half of the rates in the United States, and, if opinion polls are to be believed, most Japanese wives feel better off than their American counterparts. Of children born in Japan, 1.1 percent were to unwed mothers; in the United States the figure was 30.1 percent. Infant mortality is the lowest in the world and longevity, to age 81, the highest. Japan also has much less crime, despite "dangerous seventeen-year-olds." Big cities are safe at night. Drugs are not a serious problem. Handguns were banned with predictable results: in 2000 23 persons were killed by guns in Japan; in the United States the figure was more than 10,000. Of every 100,000 persons, 37 are in jail in Japan; in the United States, 519. Though housing is crowded and social pressures great, the society overall is healthy.

Contemporary Japanese culture also has strengths and weaknesses. Many praise the continuing vitality of the Japanese traditional arts of poetry, painting, pottery, paper-making, tea ceremony, flower arrangement, and Kabuki and Nō drama. Masters of these arts produce works of great beauty and are sometimes honored as "Living National Treasures." Others argue that many of these arts have lost their original spirit and become fossilized. Schools of tea ceremony and flower arrangement, they contend, are little more than genteel diploma mills, producing huge revenues for the families that run them.

Japanese architecture and gardens, at their best, have effected a transition from the simple beauty of traditional styles with their use of natural materials to the recreation of the same esthetic using modern forms and techniques. Foreign architects flock to study in Japan, and Japanese architects have a worldwide clientele. Yet, at the same time, much of the former charm of Japanese cities has been destroyed by a lack of zoning laws, indiscriminate building, and an excess of automobiles. Even Kyoto, apart from pockets of beauty, has become a jumble of oddly styled houses and ugly concrete buildings surmounted by television antennae and a tangle of electrical wires. Its lesser temples and shrines, the only equivalent to public parks, often double as kindergartens and parking lots, complete with vending machines.

Criticism notwithstanding, in literature, drama, painting, and dance the prewar tradition of vigorous experiments with new or hybrid forms continues. The Japanese awareness of nature, so evident in postwar films like Kurosawa's *Rashōmon* or *The Seven Samurai*, carries over to the photography in Japanese National Television dramas and nature shows. More recently, films by Itami Jūzō—*Tampopo* and *A Taxing Woman*—and Suo Masayuki—*Shall We Dance,*—combined off-beat humor with biting satire. Symphony orchestras in Japan's major cities play Mozart and Stravinsky as well as native compositions by Takemitsu with haunting passages on the Japanese flute and zither. Clothing designers compete in Tokyo, New York, and Paris. College students form rock bands, listen to jazz, and read Japanese science fiction along with the writings of serious novelists.

JAPAN: A FUTURE PERSPECTIVE

Where will changes come in the future and what will be their source? Despite problems such as an ageing population that will require considerable adjustments, Japanese society seems stable and well integrated and not a likely candidate for sudden upheavals. The present state of Japanese culture, as well, seems to satisfy most Japanese. The marketplace for ideas and cultural products is open and varied. An outside observer may note that Christianity is more a part of modern Western culture than is Buddhism or Shinto in modern Japan. On census returns only four fifths of one percent of Japanese identify themselves as Christian. The vast majority see themselves as Buddhist or Shinto or both. But for most, their professed affiliations mainly involve participation in weddings, funerals, or other obligatory rituals; only a minority have deep religious beliefs that help shape their self-identity. This disconnect with tradition, however, does not seem to concern most Japanese.

For now, Japan's diplomacy is weak, but its foreign relations are in good shape. The end of the Cold War has led to improved relations with China and Russia. Japan is not directly involved in the tensions surrounding Taiwan and the two Koreas. In geopolitical terms, it can be argued that Japan is militarily weak and strategically vulnerable in a part of the world in which China, Russia, and the United States are nuclear powers. In this situation it is clear that militarism of any stripe is no longer a live option. Of course, Japan has the capacity to become an instant nuclear power, but no incentive to do so (and many incentives not to) as long as it continues to trust in its Security Treaty with the United States. Under these conditions, its relations with the world seem destined to remain largely commercial; peace and free trade will remain the pillars of its foreign policy.

Newspapers are famously opportunistic. During the 1980s Western papers described the Japanese as economic supermen; more recently they describe them as weak-willed and inept. Both views distort and lack historical perspective. At the end of World War II no one dreamed that Japan, an island nation the size of Montana and with few natural resources, would become the second largest economy in the world. But its skilled labor force, talented managers, and pragmatic political leaders made it happen. The stagnation of the 1990s raises the question of whether it can maintain this ranking. Some Japanese say it must. Others say it does not really matter. The only real test of a nation is the wellbeing of its people, and the Japanese, despite current problems, enjoy a high standard of living, political freedoms, a rich and varied culture, and a stable and safe society. Japan will eventually recover from its slump. Even if its ranking slips a notch or two, its educated people and huge productive capacity will maintain these conditions for decades to come.

Japan's political future is often debated. In 1945 the prospects for representative government in Japan were hazy. The Occupation view was that the Japanese were given to militarism and still "half-feudal" in their values. The vigor of its reforms stemmed from its determination to eradicate these traits. After the war, and even today, Japanese liberals often contend that the notions of freedom, equality, and human rights are insufficiently rooted in Japan. They worry about the resurgence of nationalism and the emergence of right-wing figures such as Ishihara Shintarō, the governor of Tokyo. They point out that modern Japan has produced no Washington, Jefferson, Lincoln, or Roosevelt. When newspaper editorials call for forceful leaders to rescue Japan from economic stagnation, they look back to the "men of Meiji," the tough-minded ex-samurai who built the modern state, or to Yoshida Shigeru, the "one-man" of the early postwar era. No editorial mentions Ōkuma, Katō, or Inukai, the prewar party politicians.

That said, the case for optimism remains strong. Fukuzawa Yukichi wrote in 1872 that "Heaven does not create one person above and another below; all are born equal." Several ex-samurai leaders broke with the Meiji government during the 1870s and 1880s, formed political parties, and worked to establish representative institutions. As these institutions developed through the 1920s, Japan came fairly close to establishing a true parliamentary system. Minobe Tatsukichi and Yoshino Sakuzō advanced arguments in favor of democracy. Socialists of various persuasions stressed equality and the need for greater welfare. The prewar legacy may not simply be dismissed as militarist.

Indeed, the Occupation reforms succeeded because they built on prewar representative institutions. After Japan regained sovereignty in 1952, successive governments upheld most of the reforms and Japanese saw them as timely and beneficial, and not as something foisted on them by an occupying power. Social conditions are also more advanced. Unlike the prewar, Japan today has a large, educated middle class —a necessary base for representative government. The large swing vote in elections rests on this class and reflects its new political maturity. Not least important is the constitutional right of the majority party, or coalition, in the lower house of the Diet to form the government. During the 1930s, we recall, the right to name a prime minister was exercised by "the men around the throne." The militarists came to power through this loophole, despite control of the Diet by centrist-conservative parties. Some politicians today propose to revise the postwar Constitution, but their intended revisions will neither diminish the importance of the lower house nor affect the centrality of elections.

In the spacious entrance hall of the Diet building in Tokyo there are four pedestals. Three are occupied by bronze statues of men who contributed to parliamentary government in Japan: Itagaki Taisuke, who founded Japan's first political party, Ōkuma Shigenobu, who founded the second party and was twice prime minister, and Itō Hirobumi, author of the Meiji Constitution and four-time prime minister. The fourth pedestal is empty. It is reserved for a future hero of representative government.

REVIEW QUESTIONS

1. In some respects postwar parliamentary politics resembles the politics of the 1920s, but the differences are more important. Discuss.

2. What accounted for Japan's rapid economic growth in the postwar era, and why did it slow down and then almost stop?

3. "In two more decades Japan's postwar history will be as long as its prewar modern history, yet the changes of the prewar seem far more fundamental." Discuss.

4. Any change in a society must be anchored to something that does not change, for if everything changed at once, the society would fall apart. Do you agree? How would you apply your answer to postwar Japan?

5. What are the long-term American interests in the western Pacific? What are Japan's interests in East Asia? What should be the goals of U.S. policy toward Japan?

SUGGESTED READINGS

G. BERNSTEIN, *Haruko's World: A Japanese Farm Woman and Her Community* (1983). A study of the changing life of a village woman in postwar Japan.

T. BESTOR, *Neighborhood Tokyo* (1989). A portrait of contemporary urban life in Japan.

G. L. CURTIS, *The Logic of Japanese Politics: Leaders, Institutions, and the Limits of Change* (1999).

G. L. CURTIS, ed., *New Perspectives on U.S.–Japanese Relations* (2000). A multi-author work.

P. DUUS, ed., Vol. 6 of *The Cambridge History of Japan: the Twentieth Century* (1988). Essays by a variety of scholars.

S. GARON, *Molding Japanese Minds: The State in Everyday Life* (1997). Regulation by the state in prewar and postwar Japan of welfare, prostitution, personal savings, religious cults, and sexual politics.

T. S. GEORGE, *Minamata: Power, Policy, and Citizenship in Postwar Japan* (2001). A study of the unfolding of the drama of the Minamata industrial poisoning as it illustrates local, prefectural, and national politics.

A. GORDON, ed., *Postwar Japan as History* (1993). A multi-author volume.

H. HIBBETT, ed., *Contemporary Japanese Literature: An Anthology of Fiction, Film, and Other Writing Since 1945* (1977). A lively collection of translations of postwar fiction.

C. JOHNSON, *MITI and the Japanese Miracle: The Growth of Industrial Policy, 1925–1975* (1982). On the role of a government ministry.

Y. KAWABATA, *The Sound of the Mountain* (1970). A splendid translation of a moving novel by the first Japanese author to win a Nobel Prize.

J. NATHAN, *Sony, the Private Life* (1999). A very readable account of the growth of Sony Corporation as seen in the personalities and business decisions of its founders.

D. OKIMOTO, *Between MITI and the Market* (1989). A discussion of the respective roles of government and private enterprise in Japan's postwar growth.

S. PHARR, *Losing Face: Status Politics in Japan* (1990).

S. PHARR, *Media and Politics in Japan* (1996).

E. O. REISCHAUER, *The Japanese Today* (1995). A readable account of various facets of contemporary Japan.

E. F. VOGEL, *Japan as Number One: Lessons for America* (1979). While dated and overly sanguine, this sociological analysis of the sources of Japan's economic growth is sharp and insightful.

Index